P9-ECO-705

Acknowledgment to Our Teachers

We give thanks to the teachers who have
influenced our path—the illumination
they have brought to our lives is invaluable
and we are eternally grateful.

THE AWAKENED WOMAN'S GUIDE
TO EVERLASTING LOVE

THE AWAKENED WOMAN'S GUIDE
TO EVERLASTING LOVE

LONDIN ANGEL WINTERS
JUSTIN PATRICK PIERCE

SACRED

2018

© 2018 by Sacred Existence

Sacred Existence, LLC., Los Angeles, CA 90066

Awakened Woman's Guide™ is a trademark of Sacred Existence, LLC.

All rights reserved. No part of this book may be reproduced in any form or by any means, electronic or mechanical, including photocopying, recording, or by any information storage and retrieval system, without permission in writing from the authors and publisher.

The authors of this book do not dispense medical advice or prescribe the use of any technique as a form of treatment for physical, emotional, or medical problems without the advice of a physician, either directly or indirectly. The intent of the authors is only to offer information of a general nature to help you in your quest for physical, emotional and spiritual well-being. In the event that you use any of the information in this book for yourself, which is your constitutional right, the authors and the publisher assume no responsibility for your actions.

Edited by James Ranson
Cover design by Rahul Panchal
Interior design by Justin Patrick Pierce

Cataloging-in-Publication Data is on File at the Library of Congress

Published 2018

ISBN: 978-0-9863942-4-9

May this book serve
the women and men of this world,
and help them come to better understand
and love one another.

Table of Contents

Conclusion

Special Sections

PREFACE

Welcome

We are excited to journey with you into creating and sustaining ever-lasting love. Justin and I wrote this book from the depths of our hearts and we hope to inspire you to look into the depths of your heart as you read it.

This book will help you apply the principles of sacred intimacy to the modern relationship. In it, you will learn how to thrive in a relationship, so you may experience the love and ravishment you deserve in this lifetime.

Justin and I have dedicated our lives to the study and practice of sacred intimacy. We aren't therapists, nor are we doctors. We could be called yogis, spiritual seekers or, as we prefer, students and teachers of love. We don't teach from hypotheticals. We teach from experience, formal practice and study, combined with years of being in a loving and thriving relationship with each other. Through living in a sacred relationship for nearly a decade, we have dedicated each and every day to doing whatever practice it takes to keep the flow of love and passion present. As many couples know, a long-term relationship has a way of drying things up. The best practices are the ones which stand the test of time, and build the relationships that work throughout the years. These are the practices we teach because these are the ones we live.

This exploration is a spiritual one, designed for those who are eager to dive deeply into the practice of sacred intimacy. In addition to sharing helpful practices and mindsets, we will invite you to take a good, honest look at how you show up in a relationship. For this reason, you may find this book challenging at times. It may bring up strong emotions around love, loss and past relationship dynamics.

If this happens, remember to have compassion for yourself, to be gentle and to know you are walking into sensitive territory. If you find yourself being triggered at any point, soften your heart and keep breathing. Breathing will help the feelings move through you. If you need a moment to pause and digest the content, allow yourself to do so. This will help you come back to the teachings fresh and ready for more.

Although the concepts explored in this book are written from a heterosexual perspective, we welcome readers of all sexual orientations to land themselves in the material. The principles taught here are of value to anyone interested in deepening an intimate relationship.

Message to the Awakened Woman

Justin and I wrote this book for the awakened woman—a woman who is understanding life on new terms, who has achieved the same things men are used to achieving, but might feel unmet by career alone, and longs for deeper love.

She may even feel at odds with herself. One part of her—the purpose-driven part—has been totally liberated and loves that nothing is stopping her from creating anything she wants, but her heart stands divided because the other part of her—the love-driven part—stares at the ceiling at night crying for more. It longs to be cherished, seen and claimed.

This book is for the next generation of women who are stepping into sharing power with men. These women have a choice: they'll either model patriarchal trends of ruling, disembodied and dominating, or they will create something we've never seen before, where the tenderness which lives in every woman's heart becomes the thing that makes the difference.

The awakened woman cannot cut herself off from her body. Her heart won't let her. So she awakens through love. She calls in a deep man who opens her more than she can open herself. He peels back her layers, helping her find divine surrender, giving her the ability to tune more clearly into the wisdom that lies within her than she could on her own. She goes back into her power position the next day, wide open and connected to the divine, and creates something the world has never seen.

This is a powerful time in history. Women have the opportunity to step into their destiny as leaders without losing the precious love-driven side of themselves. It is the desire for love which leads them into a partnership, and it is the partnership which nourishes them as they lead. I know for myself I would not be able to stand in half of the luminescent power I hold if it wasn't for my relationship with Justin. It is not my power—it's the power of the two of us as a channel coming through me. It's not me and it's not him; it's both of us. It's the checks and balances of each other's perspectives. It's the opening we create together, an awakening that moves through each one of us, which is not possible without the other.

A revolution is on the horizon—a revolution of women in positions of influence, supported by men of consciousness—two serving as one.

This revolution starts in relationship, two beings in devotion to each other, awakening within each other: love, purpose, luminescence, power, pleasure and happiness. Imagine what will change for the whole of humanity when each and every awakened woman starts living as love, without shutting down or holding back, without compromise, and with a daily full-body yes to the call of the heart.

The way to hear that call is to ask yourself one simple question and trust the answer. The question is:

How do you need to give your love before you die?

Write down the first things that come to your heart.

Let your answer to this question guide you in embracing the teachings in this book. Let it inform your role in the revolution. Let it be your mantra. Let it be the thing that gives you the courage to live as love, *no matter what.*

Through His Eyes: Conscious Men Embracing Women of Power, by Justin

There are two types of men: the kind who feel emasculated by powerful women, and the kind who are inspired by them.

Why would a powerful, conscious man fall in love with a woman who is equally as powerful, or even more powerful than he? Because he understands it is she who will help him become the man he must become before he dies.

To step into an intimate relationship with a woman who brings an equal and complementary depth to the equation is a profound gift for any man. Men of the modern age are seeking women who have vision, influence and wisdom. They recognize these qualities as gifts just as precious as radiance and beauty. The awakened woman is a conscious man's compass. She is his passionate lover, his source of nourishment, his oracle of wisdom, his partner in crime and his wake-up call when he has drifted astray. She is his greatest ally and most challenging opponent. It is through her alone he may clearly see his own consciousness in the reflection of her love. It is her heart that ensures he does not let this lifetime slip away.

Despite this, men also recognize that being with a woman of tremendous force can lead to power struggles, with each partner asserting their will over the other. Too often in these cases, the sexual charge drains right out of the dynamic as both end up "turned off." For a modern man to enjoy being with a woman of influence, both partners must know how to navigate this tendency, guiding it toward fulfillment rather than frustration. That's what this book is here to teach you.

Historically, men and women have been taught to suppress their authentic truth in an effort to "go along to get along." While this can sustain a functional dynamic, it is kryptonite to intimacy, and it is not the solution for sustaining a passionate relationship. Rather, it is a ruse that breeds resentment over time, leaving both partners yearning for something more.

The future, by contrast, looks like conscious men embracing women of power, being gifted by their wisdom and their passion, while cultivating the ability to serve these women from a place of unshakeable consciousness. This consciousness nourishes women in a way no achievement or success ever could. Intimacy is deepened, power is shared.

To consciously dance at this highest level of union is the apex of sacred relationship. It preserves sexual attraction and gives the gift of spiritual awakening, through each partner's devotion to the other's fulfillment of love and purpose in this lifetime.

INTRODUCTION

"Do you want me to tell you something really subversive?
Love is everything it's cracked up to be.
That's why people are so cynical about it.
It really is worth fighting for, being brave for,
risking everything for. And the trouble is,
if you don't risk anything, you risk even more."

- Erica Jong, Fear of Flying -

Introduction

One of the worst things a woman can feel is a loss of love. Deep connection is what most women live for.

When the icy winds of neutrality blow their way into a woman's life, a part of her deadens.

- The part of her that lives for joy and ravishment gives way to the part that gets stuff done.
- The part that wants to be claimed by her man caves into the part that pursues self-sufficiency.
- The part that longs to be fucked open to the divine dies to the part that masters the latest vibrator.

In the deepest feminine heart, the play of love's flow determines everything. If love isn't flowing, nothing in her life feels as if it's working. A career can be a convenient distraction, but work alone won't fulfill her heart. When a woman feels unloved, she suffers. It doesn't matter how many plans she makes, romantic movies she watches or chocolates she eats—a part of her feels as if life is on hold until the flow of love is back.

A woman in this place may find herself losing confidence. Her radiance dims, her flow clogs and her color wanes. She stops taking care of herself, she starts dressing down, she feels heavy and neurotic and gets stuck in endless worries. Exercise feels impossible and she may find herself grasping for endless frothy lattes as a desperate source of energy. As her vagina dries up, she might begin to feel sex as incredibly painful or unpleasant. She watches herself slip into the shadows of aging, feeling more invisible with every passing day, no matter how young she is.

You might know these feelings well. You may have felt them before.

You may be feeling them now. I've felt them countless times myself. It sucks feeling like your life lacks the level of juicy love you've always desired it to have.

You don't have to feel this way forever.

Imagine…

• If your intimacy was your source of nourishment for showing up in the world.
• If you could attract a deep man and have him claim you for life.
• If disagreements brought you closer to your partner.
• If you had the tools to make lovemaking grow hotter over time, so 10 years in, sex was even more fulfilling than ever.
• If you felt desired and claimed beyond your surface, so aging wasn't an issue.
• If you had a partner to grow with spiritually.
• If every day you felt loved and fulfilled—both within yourself and with your partner.

And imagine if he wanted all of this as much as you.

It's not impossible. It's not even improbable. It's within your reach, right now, no matter who you are or where you are. And in the pages to follow, we will show you how to reach it. This book is about sacred relationship—how to create and sustain it, no matter how many curveballs are thrown your way.

Sacred relationship is a way of approaching intimacy where you choose to love so deeply, to give so fully, to receive so completely, that life itself takes on a new axis, an axis created by two which neither person could achieve on their own.

When we use the word "intimacy," here's what we mean:

Hot Sex. That rip-your-clothes-off impulse that happens so easily in the beginning, but seems to fade over time. We'll show you how to keep it alive no matter how long you are together.

Gooey Connection. Intimacy that is not sexual, but equally delicious, such as the feeling of walking hand-in-hand and taking in the moment so deeply that time disappears. We'll show you how to nurture the kind of bonds that are just as fulfilling fully clothed.

Fierce Love. The kind of commitment which pervades the darkest of times. You have the tools to make times of struggle bond you deeper in unconditional love. We'll show you how to use them.

Intimacy is all of it, from the purely sexual to the powerfully bonding. It is all of life and living in the unbreakable bond of eternal love.

Applying Ancient Wisdom
to Modern Relationship

You'll probably notice that the foundational concepts illustrated in this book are not new.

For example, ancient spiritual texts have spoken about the concept of polarity for thousands of years. Across multiple cultures and civilizations, we've seen spiritual teachings talk about the differences between good and evil, light and dark, masculine and feminine, consciousness and nature, yin and yang, and so on. Similarly, ancient Hindu teachings bring us Shiva and Shakti—manifestations of the united divine consciousness—each representing different sides of the same coin: one side feminine and one side masculine.

Traditionally, followers of these teachings, and of others we'll explore in these pages, dedicated their whole lives to such practices. They often sacrificed luxury and even normalcy to do so, living on the fringes of society or in meditative isolation. As a result, the teachings were also kept isolated, often made top secret and saved for the rich or devout few. Today, this obscure but powerful work is emerging into the mainstream. And as it becomes accessible to the masses, it is starting to challenge traditional roles within intimacy, helping both men and women find power, tenderness and passion which was previously hidden or inaccessible.

All this is to say what you will read here didn't originate with us. Our intention is not to claim credit for coming up with something new. Instead take these divine, ancient wisdoms and translate them into the modern, evolving relationship.

Dropping into Sacred Space

Imagine this book like a workshop for intimacy. In order to get the most out of a workshop, it's vital to prepare your body and mind before you arrive. We invite you to approach the introductory sections of this book as that preparation; they are the foundation upon which your process into deeper loving stands. They will show you exactly how to show up in body, mind and spirit to get the most out of this book.

Although this book is based on sacred intimacy, it is important to realize that its principles are not limited to the bedroom or other sexual occasions. It is our goal to teach you the universal principles of love, so each moment of your life may become an intimate communion with the divine.

However, because this is a book about cultivating sacred intimacy, it is going to include some graphic sexual content to illustrate how these teachings translate directly to the bedroom. But that doesn't mean it's going to be a traditional sex manual. At no point are we going to cover sexual positions or mechanics. There are many sources already available in this regard. We are interested in going beyond the technique and teaching you the foundational principles of true intimate connection, upon which every position and technique you could ever learn should stand. In this way, you don't even need to know about the techniques to become a world-class lover.

As you implement these teachings, you may notice your perspective toward relationships and love shifting. For this reason, we recommend you reference this book often, rather than simply reading it once and expecting to have learned everything there is to learn. You will notice each time you return to the text or review a section, you will discover new things. When you hit a new challenge, you can use the resources given here to help meet it successfully. As you encounter new issues with your partner, you can reference the practices to bring your relationship back into love. If you are single, you can read this with your future beloved in mind and get an idea of the kind of partner you want to attract and how to manifest them into reality.

Full disclosure—this material can feel intense. Past dynamics may be flying around in your head as you read. Concerns of how much there is to learn may mount. Questions about whether you will ever get it may surface. It is okay to feel overwhelmed. That's a normal and valid response. If this happens, we recommend you do something to soothe your body and heart before you continue reading. Put on a song and dance, go into nature, take a bath or drink some tea. We also suggest you keep a pen close by. You could even take this book on holiday and use it like a retreat, or try reading it with a partner, a friend or a group and create an open discussion on the topics.

Whatever you need to do, know you are touching upon one of the most basic of human desires, to be loved. Love lives at the core of our being. Studies have shown that love is as critical for a human being to thrive as food and water. For many of us, the question "Am I lovable?" is a huge trigger, and examining how we show up in a relationship can feel like a threat to our very survival.

As you go through these concepts, you may find a few directions helpful to keep in mind:

1. Give up ideas of "getting it right," and resist the impulse to criticize yourself or your partner when either of you falls short of expectations. There is no right or wrong here, there is only the practice.

2. Know that being where you are is perfect, even if you have struggled in the past. What happened then brought you to where you are now.

3. Remember sacred relationship isn't just something you do with your partner. It's also something you do with yourself, including right now reading this book and processing all that it could be unearthing for you.

4. Approach the practice from loving compassion, kindness and deep reverence for yourself and your partner. Be gentle and trust the process.

Throughout this book, you will see questions we ask you with areas to fill in your responses. We encourage you to use those questions to treat this book like a journal. The explorations we offer will enhance the journey.

Periodically, you will also see this:

*** *Breathe* ***

Each time you see it, we suggest that you do exactly that—breathe.

So much of our capacity to give and to receive love boils down to our ability to remain present, to feel fully, to soften, and to surrender into the moment, no matter how uncomfortable it feels. The most powerful way to do this is through the breath. So, when you see this:

*** *Breathe* ***

Follow these steps:
    1. Pause for a moment.
    2. Close your eyes.
    3. Inhale a deep breath.
    4. Feel it cascade down the front surface of your body as you draw it in.
    5. Allow it to soothe your heart, fill your belly and awaken the soles of your feet.

6. As you exhale, soften your body from the inside out.

7. Repeat as many times as you like.

Now that you know the drill, let's give it a shot.

*** ***Breathe*** ***

Your Owner's Manual For Intimacy

This book has four main sections. The first section introduces the mindset and background of sacred relationship, including necessary terms and definitions, foundational principles, goals and basic practices. This section is partially told through the story of our relationship's development, as the sacred intimacy teaching and training we do is based very closely on how we learned to open each other into the powerful, devoted connection we have now. We share these stories to give away what we have been blessed to enjoy, as well as to help give context to the teachings and practices we love so much.

This first section also sets the stage for the three later sections, the Three Pillars of Everlasting Love. These three pillars of presence, polarity and devotion are the foundation upon which a sacred relationship is built. Each pillar section will discuss what the pillar is, how it works, what benefits it brings when practiced, what challenges are involved with practicing it and some specific instructions on how to practice it. The first section will thus prepare you to dive deeply into the pillar sections by helping you prepare your body, mind and spirit to do so.

As you saw in the very beginning, the book is divided into two different voices. One is a combination of myself, Londin, speaking alone, and both Justin and I speaking together, and it makes up some 80% of the book. The other is Justin speaking by himself, providing a masculine perspective on various points that we (and our early readers) believed would be enhanced by it. Justin's sections will always include the phrase "Through His Eyes" in their titles, for easy reference.

We did this for two particular reasons: first, because I could not have created the relationship that inspired this book on my own. I did it with Justin. He plays an equal role in the depth and passion we enjoy. Therefore, he plays a major role in sharing our secrets with you.

Justin will help you better understand the man's perspective on sacred relating. This practice isn't about dragging your man along kicking and screaming into your dream romance, manipulating him into commitment, or hammering him into monogamy. To the contrary, we present a model of relating where power games cease, and both partners thrive inside the dynamic.

Second, we've found the best way we teach is together, with both of us contributing and sharing. And while this book isn't a live workshop, we wanted to bring as much of that teaching environment to it as possible.

One particular element of our workshops we really wanted to bring to this book was having examples of individual situations, like the ones our workshop attendees ask us to help them work through. So, in addition to elements of our own story, we are including short interludes called "Love Conflicts" throughout the text. These interludes are all real challenges women we've worked with have experienced on their journeys to a sacred relationship. We've changed the names, of course, and taken some creative license with the descriptions, but the stories themselves—and the "Love Solutions" we helped these women find—are very real.

Finally, because practicing these teachings requires the embodiment of them, you will sometimes hear us refer to it as "yoga" or "the yoga." When we use those terms, we are not referring to the kinds of poses you would find in a yoga class. We are referring to taking the practices beyond the mind and putting them into action. It's important to recognize that the practices here do not deliver change if you simply understand them as concepts. You must embody the teachings themselves to experience the desired results. This is what we mean when we say "yoga" or the "Yoga of Intimacy™."

A Note to the Single Reader

At this point, you may be wondering, "What if I don't have a part. How can I practice sacred relationship if I don't have a relationship practice it in?" If you are single, don't worry. This book is for you just as much as it is for anyone who has a partner at the moment.

Sacred relationship is not about an outcome. It's not saying to yourself, "Oh, I have a partner now, so I'm ready to live these principles." Rather, it's a way of life that you can start practicing now. That practice will call your partner in and prepare you for the moment they arrive, so that when they do, you are already well practiced in the art of sacred relating, living the exact behaviors which keep that love thriving.

Sacred relationship is about finding the well of juicy love that lives at your core and letting it nourish you, pour out from you and overflow into the world. It's about un-guarding your heart, removing the shackles of self-suppression, and bringing the authentic you to each and every moment, so one day a partner looks over and thinks, "Hello, soulmate!" It's about letting the wisdom of your profound connection to the divine inspire your heart and guide your life path, fully enraptured in body, mind and spirit—and call in the love you want from there.

Most of all, it's a path where you let go of recreating the limiting patterns of old wounds which tend to close the heart and repel love. Instead, drop your guard and love like you've never been hurt…no matter what.

Think back to the way you were long before you ever felt the sting of rejection, shame or betrayal: How did you love before you ever knew hurt? What were you unafraid to give, show or be?

Write down what you remember.

Before we knew pain, we loved from innocence. Once we have experienced hurt, we must make a conscious choice to open to love again. The awakened woman loves because she chooses to live fully.

Sacred relating is about unleashing this place in you, the one you just identified above, and bringing it as a gift in the way you walk through life. When you love at this level and live from this place, guess what? You call deeper partners into your life. You call your partner into your life. And while you work on that practice, you also build a sacred relationship with yourself, so even when you are single, you're never truly alone.

LAYING THE FOUNDATION
FOR EVERLASTING LOVE

1

Our Story

While today Justin and I enjoy a deeply fulfilling relationship and travel the world teaching the practice of sacred intimacy, it wasn't always this way for us. We didn't catch each other's eye from across the room and glide into a sacred union. We didn't land in love right off the bat, or even start dating right away. Quite the contrary, the journey before meeting was rough, and our coming together was one of adversity, ups and downs and lots of patience. Now it's easy to look at what we have and think it was fate, destiny or some other delicious gift which brought us together. It wasn't. Instead, it was a commitment to show up to the most difficult moments with open hearts and honest communication that drew us closer. We loved each other through tough times at the start and we stay through difficult times now, and year after year, our love deepens as a result.

Life Before Justin: Blessed with Success and Unlucky in Love

Prior to meeting Justin, my early years were a fierce commitment toward achievement. After graduating in the top 10% of my class at Northwestern University, I spent my 20s and 30s manifesting success. Most notably, I won an Emmy, created financial freedom, headed a travel network and won a figure competition. It was as if, whatever I set out to do, I had the Midas touch—except when it came to love.

All of my awards, money and success were great, but they did little to soothe the gnawing hunger that lived deep within my heart. Without true love, none of it felt truly fulfilling. I wanted a soulmate, and I couldn't seem to find one no matter how hard I tried. And it wasn't that I couldn't find men. I was attracting plenty of suitors; they just didn't offer me the kind of relationship I wanted. I wondered what was wrong with me and why I couldn't seem to make anything work. I doubted my ability to pick a man and ping-ponged between never wanting to date again and not being able to fall in love soon enough.

The lowest of lows was a failed marriage in my early 30s.

Within a few months of getting married, my ex-husband and I fell into being powerful business partners and not much else. Even when we would go away for a weekend together, we didn't have sex. Or, if we did, it was pretty lame and based on renting a "movie" to get us in the mood. We weren't making love, we were following along to a movie, working out some sexual tension. It was beyond depressing.

Soon after, my husband became increasingly cold and rude to me. He stopped showing affection. He clung to the opposite side of the bed, or slept in a different bed most nights. It became harder and harder to get along, and after a while, I couldn't decide whom I wanted to kill more, myself or him.

One time we got into a fight on date night at the movies and he stormed out of the theater. After the movie ended, I waited outside the theater for an hour, finally realizing he had driven home without me, literally abandoning me. I had to call a cab to get home. That cab ride was one of the lowest moments of my life.

After several more of these heartbreaking episodes, we decided to divorce. Packing up my three-bedroom home and trying to cram all my shit into a studio apartment, I definitely felt unlucky in love.

My next serious relationship didn't go much better, but for completely different reasons. I went from being with a man who was emotionally abusive but full of power, to being with a man who was emotionally supportive but powerless. He was full of love and void of money. I'm embarrassed to admit that I went for a guy who, at nearly 50 years old, was still living with his mother. He always had excuses for being broke, and for a long time I bought right into them. He had broken his back in an accident and taught himself to walk again. He was a gifted mystic and mentor to many celebrities in LA. While I was enamored of his unique set of skills, I completely overlooked his incompetence to handle money, business and all things practical. I lapped up his love like a starving cat laps up milk.

I felt safe with him and seen by him, and it was a salve for my battered heart. The accident had rendered him unable to become erect, but it didn't matter. He made up for it with the most impressive sexual skills in every other area. Coming off the dry spell of my marriage, it was exactly what I needed.

Eventually though, it became tiring when I began to see why he couldn't get it together. He couldn't manage money or motivate himself to work. He literally would choose spending time with me over showing up to jobs. Watching him make one poor decision after another, I began to see that his impotence extended much further than the bedroom.

Suddenly all of that good loving he was giving me felt hollow. The appeal of his doting dried up. Deep down, that wasn't the arrangement I wanted. Playing the breadwinner was not my happily ever after. This guy and I were actually competing to be the pampered one in the relationship—and he was winning by a long shot. I had to get out or I would forever sentence myself to being his caretaker. So I ended it.

After this and a long series of uninteresting dating experiences, I found myself wondering, "What now?" and getting no clear answers.

I began to wonder if love could ever work out for me.

This was a turning point in my life. It was this crossroads that led me to the path I am on now and led me to Justin. The pain of all of these relationship dynamics led to an intense vision quest where I threw out everything I thought I knew about love and I started from scratch. In this journey, I discovered what it takes to stop the pattern, to stop the flip-flop between either running the show or being run over by it. I finally learned how to stop repelling true love and call toe-curling ravishment into my life. And it was from there that I attracted Justin into the picture.

Enter Justin: Not Exactly Love at First Sight

Believe it or not, when I first met Justin, it didn't go so well. In fact, if you witnessed my first year of knowing Justin, you'd be surprised to find out we ended up in a relationship at all. It certainly didn't feel like we were headed in that direction.

First of all, there is a huge age gap. I am 14 years older than Justin. Second, there was his stage in life. Justin was just 23 years old when we met and he had just arrived in LA. He was as far from the mindset of long-term commitment as it gets. If you've ever had a crush on someone who wasn't ready for a relationship, you can probably feel how difficult this was for me.

There was no doubt we had a deep soul bond—it was evident from the start. There was no doubt we were crazy about each other—we wanted to spend every minute together. There was no doubt the heart connection and sexual chemistry were off the charts—they were, for both of us. But even all of that juicy goodness was not enough to inspire Justin to be exclusive with me in the beginning. See, Justin is a purpose-driven being at his core. So no matter how amazing our dynamic felt, it wasn't enough to sway him from his mission, which at that point involved making a name for himself in business and playing the field romantically. I, in contrast, am a love-driven being, so as soon as a man rocks my world, I'm all in.

My preference was we would start our life together immediately. In my mind, what else was there to know? We were soul mates. But Justin wasn't there yet. So as hard as it was, I didn't impose my love-driven agenda on him. I didn't give him an ultimatum to get on my plan or else. Instead, I honored the track he was on. I honored his focus on mission, knowing that his strong sense of self was part of what I loved about him. It had its ups and downs, and to be honest, it was fucking hard at times. But because I was steeped in sacred practice, I kept my heart open, my feelings transparent and, despite the ache, I did the best I could to show up authentic in each and every moment.

One very long and heart-wrenching year later, Justin came to me and told me he was in for the long haul! That moment was one of the happiest moments of my life. Despite the massive age difference, despite his preferring more single time, despite my wincing from the pain of his not choosing me right away, we persevered with each other, listening more to the heart than the protestations of our minds and logic.

I tell you this for a very important reason. Justin did not walk into my life as the knight in shining armor he later became. I did not carelessly land in a fairy tale. But I do feel as though I'm living in a fairy tale now. And that to me is the power of the secrets we will share. Without the practices you will hear in this book, I would have closed my heart, fled the scene and missed out on the love of my life.

Through His Eyes: Why I Chose Relationship, by Justin

As a purpose-driven man, I am most deeply fulfilled through a strong sense of mission in life and the constant pursuit of freedom, in all its forms. For this reason, I did not desire to be in a relationship when I first met Londin. As much as I liked her, I was dating many women and felt a committed relationship would be a distraction. However, as I got to know Londin better, I realized she would help me become the man I knew I wanted to be. Once I saw this, it felt natural to let the other "options" (aka women) go and offer her my commitment. Without that distinction, which made this relationship seem so much different from the rest, I would have never been interested.

I was young when we first met—early twenties. Londin was winning fitness competitions, and I was some punk trainer at a gym. While I was an unquestionably spiritual person at that point in my life, I kept my spirituality locked up, hidden away, as something I believed I would never share with anyone—or if I did, they would never understand. As a result, I imagine my M.O. on the surface was probably quite similar to that of every other 20-something male who had just moved out to LA: partying, getting paid and getting laid. I had a tendency to wear this part of my persona on my sleeve, and when Londin and I first crossed paths, she probably took one look at me and thought "douche." Looking back, I'm certain I would've thought the same.

Despite my shallow ways in the beginning, somehow Londin was able to see through to my heart, and find a human being behind the facade of bad habits.

As Londin alluded to above, it wasn't until I recognized I was more capable of achieving both purpose and freedom inside of a relationship, as opposed to without one, that I was willing to claim Londin for life. It was then I began to hold my relationship in the highest regard. The bond between us grew as something that was real, raw and honest—something that felt hard to find in the Los Angeles dating pool. I wasn't forced into the relationship, but it became something I chose when I realized this woman was on board for inspiring me to step into the man I always wanted to become.

Once I committed to the relationship, we began formally studying and practicing sacred intimacy together, and the growth came fast. We made a commitment to not hold back any of the good, bad or ugly parts of ourselves from one another. We used the raw honesty of the moment as an opportunity to discover how to make love out of it. Despite our union having a rough and rocky start, it was a passionate ride which would ultimately deepen our love. The next thing I knew, we were moving in together.

After being with Londin for a time, I realized it wasn't my teachers or the practice of intimacy that were accelerating my spiritual growth. It was her. She was my greatest teacher. She was the one making me into the man I have become. The practices and teachers only guided me to the point where this could become true. Ultimately, the transformation was coming through her. She had become my compass.

As Londin did and does with me, the awakened woman has the ability to help the purpose-driven man navigate his way toward becoming more conscious, trustworthy, powerful, loving and capable in every way. This is the natural impulse behind all relationship dynamics, but when done unskillfully or unconsciously, it will look like both partners nagging, complaining, fighting, rejecting and resenting each other to no end. These impulses at their core are not wrong, but a sophistication needs to be brought to their expression.

This is where the yoga comes into practice. The practices we studied taught us how to keep our hearts open, how to breathe and live the moment fully, how to not run away and, most importantly, how to not stop loving each other, despite whatever light or darkness the moment could bring. These moments were just the beginning in learning what it meant to wield our love and our relationship intentionally— being co-creators of love rather than victims or lucky beneficiaries of it. We were the ones who determined if love was going to prevail, not circumstances. Those early years proved to us that when two beings are willing to show up to the truth of the other's heart, and remain present no matter what, there is always love waiting just on the other side.

Today, Londin and I are inseparable. We are business partners, best friends and passionate lovers. It is still hard for me to believe that our initial fling would become something I would want forever. It has been through our commitment to each other and our practices that this relationship has become the fuel which drives my spiritual growth and encourages me to become the man I must be before I die. I am certain I would not have arrived here any other way.

2

When Cupid Won't Cooperate

Sacred relationship will require you to show up to moments that challenge you. It will leave you feeling vulnerable because you will be in the presence of a person from whom you cannot hide. If you are willing to show up to love, as the living embodiment of love, and allow another being to be a mirror for your heart and a shepherd for your growth, you will know what it is to live in a sacred relationship.

By no means does this happen easily or accidentally. Love is complex. And only by showing up to a love where you are so fully invested that it feels as if life itself is on the line, do you find that love is absolutely worth the fight. It really is worth risking everything for.

Sometimes, love can feel like a game that cannot be won. It seems like relationships are disposable, everyone discarding one another for the next promising option. It can feel hard to relax, hard to trust.

Other times, love is good and you are enjoying a positive relationship, but you yearn for it to go deeper. You are happy together, but you intuit that there is more to the relationship. You find yourself fantasizing about what could be. You might envision growing together spiritually, each of you the champion for the other's awakening. You might visualize life slowing down a bit where you have time in a week to enjoy long, sweet, lingering kisses and making love in ever-expanding new ways. You might wish to use the beauty of your bond to gift the world and have your love serve a larger cause. But day in and day out, you can't figure out what it would take to shift into that kind of love relationship and you wonder if it is even possible. You look around and you don't see other people having it, so you wonder if what you have is as good as it gets.

When you don't know how to create intimacy and keep passion alive, it can feel as though you are at the mercy of love's whimsy. It can feel as though Cupid really does exist and he's pointing his magic arrow in every direction but yours.

- Maybe you just got rejected and wonder if showing the real you is simply "too much" for men to handle.
- Maybe your partner just stormed out of the house after a fight and you wonder whether next time it would be easier to go along and get along.
- Maybe another dude disappeared on you after sex and you wonder if there's value to those "dating rules" that teach women to withhold intercourse for leverage.
- Maybe your man hasn't bothered with foreplay in months and your only option for sexual connection is a painfully short ram session.
- Maybe you just ended it with another man-child and wonder if your love radar is broken.
- Maybe things are actually good between you and your man, but you long to go deeper with him, and don't know how.

Maybe, like I did, you find yourself flipping from one dysfunctional dynamic all the way over to an equal, but opposite one, and feel ready to give up on love all together.

In what ways have you felt unlucky in love, or craved more from your love life?

Write down your response.

Take heart. There is hope. As you heard, I faced some bleak and hopeless experiences, more than I've taken the space to convey here. If I was able to take my radiant power back, so can you. If I was able to find true love, so can you. If I was able to experience love continuing to deepen, so will you. And the guide to help you take your first step is in your hands right now.

If you can see the problem, you can fix the problem. So let's look at the problem.

Dynamics of Dysfunction

Without a roadmap, love can feel like a bona fide minefield. When our hearts are on the line, all of our most embarrassing habits emerge because love itself is the biggest trigger of them all. It ignites our wounds, fears and defenses—the ones that we keep nice and quiet at the start of a relationship. In our private coaching practice, Justin and I are presented with all sorts of examples of this minefield. The most common patterns we see are:

Serial Dating
You may fall into this category if you can never seem to find Mr. Right. You are eternally single because no one ever measures up to your standards. You say things like, "There are no good men," but never give any man more than a date or two to prove you wrong.

Relationship Cycling
This is you if you jump from one short-term relationship to the next. You meet a new guy. It brings constant texting, sexy dates and tons of attention. And then..."something happens." He stops pursuing you and the crush fizzles. You have no idea why he vaporized. So you go out to find another, because maybe the next one will be the one that works...or the one after him.

Lady Boss Earning Respect, but Losing Love
Maybe you have found power in your career, but can't seem to fit back into the intimacy model. While you feel respected in the work world, you may feel invisible in the dating pool, seeing men favor bimbos and thinking, "What the hell?!" You're left wondering if you'll ever feel ravished again, and your heart aches for a man who can meet you and isn't weakened by your power.

Powering Through a Sexless Marriage
This is you if you've landed in a marriage that's become so functional,

it feels like you are the CEO rather than the Queen of Hearts. Whether this means you run a household, raise kids or manage a business with your partner, it feels like all work and no play. You and your partner may enjoy mutual respect and good communication, but you are dying inside. If you dare to slow down for one moment and feel your situation, you might scream.

Jockeying for Power

When your dynamic thrives on never-ending conflict, you know you're stuck in power games. Extreme lows are matched perfectly with the ecstatic highs of make-up sex. Addicted to the intensity, you unconsciously fabricate drama against your own best judgment. While the relationship may be thrilling, you often feel as if you must choose between your love life and your sanity.

Playing it Safe with a Disempowered Man

Maybe you settled for the "good guy" so you didn't have to suffer yet another "bad boy." You chose him because you wanted a safe man. The problem is the only reason he feels safe is because he's suppressing his power. As a result, he suffers from a mountain of insecurities and lacks direction in life. The good guy, for all his nurturing qualities, begins to feel weak. You might even feel unsafe because you can't count on him. After a while, you find yourself yearning for a man you respect who feels like a dependable leader and a force you can relax into.

Tolerating an Untrustworthy Man

Your man may be so directionless and bad with money that he feels untrustworthy, leaving you to step up and be responsible for him. Maybe he's so wishy-washy about commitment that you can't relax into the relationship. Or maybe you picked the "bad boy." He's a super-hot lover, but outside of the bedroom, he lets you down constantly. All of these are iterations of not being able to trust your man, therefore never being able to relax into the connection.

Depleting Yourself through Over-Giving

You bend over backward to give your man everything you can, but it feels like a one-way street. He loves you doing things for him, but everything is on his terms. He takes you for granted, and calls on you only when his tank hits empty. You want his love so desperately, that you hesitate to ask him for what you need. The energetic imbalance drains you of your radiance.

Clinging to Stability

Maybe your relationship is great and you enjoy a lot of peace and harmony…but you're starting to feel more like roommates than passionate lovers. You got here because you value harmony so much you refuse to express anything unpleasant. You never rock the boat, and the side effect of all that suppression is a complete loss of passion. You wonder if you will ever be able to reclaim the sensual excitement you enjoyed when you first met.

Any of these sound familiar?

Here's the good news: you can learn to solve any of these issues through the practice of sacred relating. Whether you need to discover and shift a part of you that is driving men away, figure out how to have both career and intimacy, escape drama, reignite dying passion, inspire your man to step up, or just take something good and make it amazing, sacred relationship practice, which we call the Yoga of Intimacy™ (or "yoga" for short), can help you get there.

So let's start with the root problem behind all of these dysfunctions: no one ever really taught us how to love. Think about it—where do most of us learn anything about love? Not in school. For most of us, our best shot at learning how to love comes first from observing our parents, then from reading sex tip columns in magazines and watching romance movies.

If we learned from our parents, we may have learned to either fight like hell or stifle every unpleasant feeling. This makes us think that love is a battle. If we learned from sex tip columns, we may think the perfect blow job will get his approval. This leads us to think we need to earn love—or trade for it. If we learned from movies, we learned that every woman has a Mr. Right waiting around a corner. This prompts us to wait for him to show up, and then be discouraged when he either doesn't or isn't perfect when he does. None of these "teachers" actually prepare us for the relationship we desire.

Even therapy can be of limited use here. In therapy, we learn to talk out and analyze our problems and create agreements. While that can be extremely helpful in many ways, it encourages couples to meet mind to mind, failing to address putting energy back into the body. So it often ends up making the relationship workable logistically but uninteresting sexually. Few modalities teach the actual physical embodiment of unbridled loving—what we call "the yoga." We are interested in teaching you the yoga, because the yoga is what creates the felt experience of unconditional love and hot passion. It is the foundation of everlasting love.

The Unicorn We're All Looking For

For many of us, the desire for a loving relationship feels as primary as our craving for food and water. It is a magnetism which beckons us.

By the forces of nature, we feel ourselves pulled toward a kind of relationship we cannot find in our family, friends or mentors. It is a quality of love with a different texture entirely. It tastes both sweet and sour, and pries us open in trembling ecstasy and heart-wrenching agony.

Its complexity is its magnetism because deep down, we yearn to awaken beyond fantasy, to love without condition and to hold nothing back. We seek total surrender to something that is much larger than self, because that is the ultimate realization of love. And the best way to find that experience is to show up to a soul partner in deep loving, day in and day out, without withdrawing, no matter what.

This is the unicorn we all seek, whether we realize it or not. And it is the sacred practice we invite you to step into as you read the pages of this book.

But as it turns out, no one knows how to love perfectly all the time, every time. It's just not possible. Even the greatest saints and sages were loved by some and vilified by others.

All we can do is attempt to give our love the best we can, so that the person standing in front of us is served and made better for it. It doesn't have to be perfect. Even when we think it's perfect, sometimes it just doesn't come across that way. There will be many times when our best attempts to love will actually cause others heartache, disappointment or even pain.

What we must realize is this polarity of seemingly opposing forces is the true nature of love. It is both within conflict and resolve, agony and ecstasy, right and wrong, darkness and light where love is found. With this awareness, our understanding of love matures. We understand love is present even when the moment is painful. Even in the face of conflict and loss, we realize we still have access to love because the truth of love is that it includes everything from dark to light.

Opening to love is a matter of opening no matter what. And once this becomes our yoga, we have access to love at all times, no matter what is happening on the exterior. Apply this to a relationship with another person, and now you have the key which unlocks love despite any disagreement, loss of trust or a painful moment.

*** **Breathe** ***

An Invitation into Sacred Relationship

Now that we've named some of the relationship dysfunctions you may be dealing with and their root causes, we'd like to invite you into the Yoga of Intimacy™ as a path to creating a sacred relationship.

So what is a sacred relationship? Let's start with what it is not.

A sacred relationship is not something that is fixed or absolute. It has no final destination. It's a way of life. Most importantly, sacred relating is not pushing your own agenda. It's not seducing someone to get laid, acting agreeable to be loved, or manipulating your partner to get your way.

Anytime we give from a self-focused agenda, it's a manipulation.

Imagine a woman who wants to be loved by a man so badly that she gives more than she is ready to give, and feels violated when he takes her gifts and runs. Imagine a man who bends over backwards to accommodate his woman's frivolous demands in hopes of getting into her pants. Imagine a wife who makes a beautiful meal, lights candles, turns on music, and puts on a sexy dress to get her husband "in the mood," then feels irritated when he comes home tired after a long day and barely has the energy to look at her.

These are not acts of love. They are acts of self-service, manipulations to get someone else to respond to you the way you want. The woman wants to be claimed, the man wants sex, and the wife wants attention. None of them are giving out of devotion to their partners. All of them are giving to get back.

To love without bargains and give without conditions is a different matter entirely. It is to show up as love because you are love. It is your essential nature. When we reclaim unbridled loving and approach intimacy to share our love with others—not because we desperately need it, but because we are it—the relationship becomes something sacred.

- It is showing up for the other, no matter what.
- It is real, raw and honest loving—from fierce to tender, bringing whatever opens the other to the revelation of truth.
- It is calling each other forth, inspiring greatness.
- It is loving without conditions.
- It is devotion to your beloved's spiritual awakening.

From this orientation, relationship enters the realm of devotion. Every breath is another opportunity to give and receive love. Boundless love is available to all of us in every moment. It is just a matter of knowing where to look.

Now we recognize it may be strange, heavy, triggering, overwhelming and emotional to step so fully into authentic loving. Like a good yoga class, it will stretch you in ways which feel uncomfortable at first.

But as these principles become a practice for you, the newfound depth you will experience in daily life makes the stretch more than worth it. You will experience feeling more "met" than ever before. You will find yourself opening, growing and benefiting in ways you've never imagined. And this will happen not just romantically, but across all areas of your life.

3

The Three Pillars of Everlasting Love

The three pillars are the magic upon which every deep, intimate interaction relies. Anyone who has experienced profound moments of intimacy has probably discovered one or more of the pillars organically or accidentally. The idea here is we are doing it consciously, again and again. To intentionally evoke deep moments of intimacy, we must develop a workable knowledge of these pillars.

The first and most important thing to know is that not one of the pillars is any more or less important than the others. They work like a three-legged stool, each bringing a key piece to create a foundation upon which everlasting love can stand. If any one of the pillars is missing, all of the best intentions and efforts in the world will eventually lead to dissonance. With all three of these pillars present, you have a powerful foundation upon which to attract and deepen a relationship over time.

The three pillars of sacred intimacy are:
1. Presence
2. Polarity
3. Devotion

They don't have to be learned or practiced in order, but we have found that beginning with presence as a foundation first helps establish depth. From depth, polarity is added to the mix to induce excitement and invite rapture. Then we bring in devotion, which allows your love to withstand the test of time.

That being said, there are aspects of each that are strengthened and deepened by the other two. As you read and begin practicing the Pillar of Polarity, for example, you will find your practice enhanced by your understanding of the Pillar of Presence, and your practice of presence similarly enriched by your understanding of polarity. For now, though, here's a brief introduction to each of the three.

> **Presence.** The only place we can experience the brilliance of love is in the right-now moment. In the Pillar of Presence, we surrender our stories from the past and release our projections into the future. Landing in the pristine possibilities of the "now," in full presence with our lover, we can experience the magic of relating soul to soul, and be able to feel each encounter ripe with newness.

> **Polarity.** To make the moments we spend together as juicy and delicious as we like, we turn to the Pillar of Polarity. Just because we are in a committed relationship, we do not have to sacrifice the intense heat of sexual desire, nor do we have to give up the soulmate quality of being best friends. How we keep things hot and interesting is to keep polarity present. In a dance of opposing energies, we seduce one another and liberate our greatest erotic exchange.

> **Devotion.** The Pillar of Devotion takes the inherent challenges of long-term relationships from adversarial to magical. It provides the glue for all of this to work. For it is only through releasing our self-serving agendas and coming at a relationship from dedication to awakening our partner's greatness that we ever truly know fulfillment in love. As long as we are focused on self, we will feel unmet by love and relationship. Loving is never about getting the thing we think we want. Rather, it is about giving that

thing which we desire most in love, without expectation. When we learn how to do this, we know our power as lover. We know fulfillment in love. When two people do this for each other, they experience the beauty of sacred relating.

With these three pillars at play, we have the opportunity to enjoy the magic of love for a lifetime. When difficulty arises, it doesn't have to shut us down. Instead, it can lead to ferocious lovemaking and an unbreakable bond.

PILLAR I: PRESENCE

"The most precious gift we can offer others is our presence.
When mindfulness embraces those we love,
they will bloom like flowers."

- Thich Nhat Hanh -

Introduction to the Pillar of Presence

In Pillar I, we cultivate the ability to land in the right-now moment. We explore what it is to become present not just in the mind, but in the body as well. This is important because it is the foundation upon which passion thrives.

Presence is the only place you can experience feeling "met." If you never take the time to learn how to land fully in the now, you will struggle to feel met by life and relationship. Presence lays the groundwork for deep intimate connection. Without it, everything will feel shallow and subtly disappointing.

For love to fully saturate the moment, both partners must land exclusively in the now.

If you are obsessing on old hurts, stewing in future concerns, or caught up in distractions, your attention is preoccupied, and you're unable to give and receive presence fully. Similarly, the way you hold your body can enhance or degrade your experience of presence. If you are guarded, closed, restricting breath or avoiding eye contact, you are avoiding presence. Anytime we cannot meet the moment in body or mind, we actively deny our partner the full force of our love. We subconsciously sabotage deep, intimate connection. And that is one of the most painful things we can do to ourselves and those we love.

In this section, we'll explore the following aspects of presence:

- Why presence is the antidote to feeling unmet in relationship.
- How the destiny of your relationship depends on your ability to show up to the right-now moment.
- How presence is the key to falling in love all over again.

• Several helpful practices to capture your partner's undivided attention.

• Why the secret to being a good lover is to stay juicy in your body and authentic in your expression.

• Five things which inadvertently degrade the moment, leaving us looking for love in all the wrong places.

• What presence looks and feels like in the bedroom (hint: it's amazing).

We'll complete this section with an exercise to cultivate presence with a partner to help you attract and sustain a deep and juicy relationship.

4

Presence, a Powerful Aphrodisiac

Most people don't realize what a powerful aphrodisiac presence can be.

Imagine two world-class tango dancers. The moment they step onto the floor, they drop into such deep connection that he becomes her lead and she becomes his flow. His shoulders are back, his spine is straight, and his relaxed strength gives her the confidence to fully surrender her hold of herself, sinking into his embrace. His every inhale presses her body open further than she could open herself. Every step, every breath, is uniting them as one. Together, they surrender into an intelligence beyond the individual, responding moment by moment to the subtlest stimulus and rippling sensation of two bodies as one.

To harmonize at this level with another requires the willingness to set aside the babble of the mind and drop into the sensorial language of the body. This is presence. To do this in intimacy is to love your partner by offering them your undivided attention. To do anything other than this in intimacy is to cause your partner pain. Imagine if the male tango dancer lost focus and dropped his partner on the floor. It would be a serious loss of trust. Imagine if he apologized and recovered full presence, but she couldn't get over it and refused to relax into his lead again. Now she is the one unwilling to be present. Their dance becomes stiff and hesitant as a result.

Presence goes both ways and it always involves mind and body. In our private coaching practice, Justin and I see this dynamic play out frequently for couples. It's easy to spot in the tango example, but it's not as easy to recognize when this dynamic is happening to you in real time.

Here's a real-life example:

Love Conflict #1: Susan Gets Screened Out

Susan meets up with her boyfriend Ryan for date night. She shows up at their favorite restaurant decked out and radiant, excited for a juicy time with him. However, as they dine, Ryan can't look up from his phone. Susan feels deflated as Ryan sends texts, checks email and engages with everyone else but her.

Susan's mind begins to spin, building subtle resentment as she thinks of all the times men in her life have let her down. To avoid having a meltdown and appearing weak, Susan disassociates from her body and closes her heart, which causes her interest in sex and romance to wane. She silently gives up on the moment, picks up her phone and matches Ryan in the monotony of cyber distraction. When they arrive home after dinner, she tells Ryan she's got a headache and goes to bed.

Love Solution #1: Don't Give Up on the Moment

Imagine if Susan hadn't given up on the moment. Instead of sitting in silent frustration at the restaurant, what if she had taken Ryan's preoccupation as an opportunity to practice sacred relating? What might she have done?

Susan would need to recognize that if she gives up on the moment, she gives Ryan a free pass to deny her presence. Every time she lets it slide, Ryan goes on thinking it's not a problem to be on his phone and the pattern only gets worse with time. Rather than meet him in distraction, Susan would need to fight for romance and stand by her desire for a fully-loaded date.

So let's look at that scenario: no matter how much Susan wants to shut down to avoid a confrontation, she resists the urge to pretend to "be cool" and instead feels and reveals the authentic truth of her heart to Ryan, knowing it's not weakness at all. It is the choice to love fully. She could do this with humor by teasingly confiscating his phone or she could be bolder and vulnerably show him her sadness.

If you think Susan might appear to be "too much" if she shows her feelings, think again. It is the truth of Susan's heart that awakens Ryan into presence. Done artfully and without blame, her loving demand grabs Ryan's attention, invites him back to the moment and thereby upgrades the experience both of them will have on that date...and at home after.

How many times have we been Ryan in that situation, too preoccupied by a screen to really share our presence with our partner until it's too late? And how many times have we been Susan, so offended by the denial of presence that we give up on depth and match our partner in mediocrity?

As we're learning, the fastest way to suffocate love's flow between two hearts is through an absence of presence. In our modern world, presence has become an increasingly rare commodity. With our minds chronically entangled in digital landscapes, we become a slave to every new alert and text message. At times, it can feel impossible to detach ourselves from our cell phones, close our computers or tear our eyes away from the TV screen.

The point here is that true authentic presence takes a willingness to open when you'd rather close and show your feelings when you'd rather withdraw. Your partner awakens through the truth of your heart displayed. If you can reveal to him the tender hurts rather than pretend to be unflappable, you give love a chance.

The depth of intimacy is determined by the quality of presence we bring to each moment. To give our beloved the full force of our undivided attention and the soft pulse of our unguarded heart is to make love to every molecule of their body, mind and spirit. You can do this over dinner. You can do it when combined in sexual embrace. You can do it anywhere and anytime, no matter how you may feel.

5

Presence Begins
with the Decision to Open

If we choose to bring presence into our lives, it starts with the decision to open rather than close.

When we close, we pinch off love's flow—game over.
When we open, we invite authentic connection—game on.

It's not always easy to open because life can be painful. The constant onslaught of hurts can make you want to shut your heart down and throw away the key. What it takes to stay present in the emotional minefield that is love, is to be willing to feel the moment without putting up your defenses. Rather than toughening up, which numbs you to the right-now moment, the practice of sacred relating invites you to stay sensitized, soft enough to feel the hurts in the first place and courageous enough to show them. This kind of responsiveness is the hallmark of the awakened woman. She is fully present, and totally transparent to the truth of the moment.

When we talk about opening, we're not talking about becoming some spiritual cheerleader who bounces around claiming, "I'm an open person, all love and light! I have no darkness!" Rather, when we say open, we mean allowing the flow of what's authentically moving through you to be seen in that moment. That could look like love and light, rage and fury, laughter, disgust or even boredom. It's about being true to the moment, letting your defenses down and being totally authentic and expressive. Love is truth. And truth has many faces—light to dark, angelic to fierce.

Keep in mind, the practice of presence is not something we learn and then turn around and demand our partner start doing. That will backfire big time. Your transformation will naturally shift your partner and it will do it in a way that keeps the sexual heat alive. If you begin telling them what to do or demanding they do these practices with you, you might get cooperation...but it will kill the sexual vibe. For now, pay attention to your side of the street and think of the decision to open as your own "asana" that you do yourself and bring to the other, thereby inspiring the relationship to a better place.

Also remember, this is not reserved for relationship only. If you begin dating from this place, as the full expression of you, you find out right away whether the partners you are dating can handle your fullness... or not. Some will find it super hot. Others will find it too much. Rather than taking this personally or as a rejection, take it as a way of sorting. If someone finds your full expression too much within the first few dates, you can pretty much guarantee they would find it way too much in a relationship. Save yourself a couple of months, and some heartache, and move on to a deeper man.

It is our ability to offer presence which creates the quality of loving we will feel in the moment. Life is not easy, and when you go through life together you are going to face some hardships—some of those struggles brought on by life, some of them brought on by each other. It is unavoidable. It is how we show up in the difficult moments that shapes the relationship.

It's critical to remember that your relationship only stays good...if it stays good. Turn against each other and it's not going to stay good. You must find a way for the two of you to navigate the inherent hardships which arise in such a way that they bring more love rather than less. This comes from staying present, no matter how heart-wrenching or confronting it feels.

For example…

> • If he is stressed from work and feels distant, how do you keep your heart from closing?

> • If you are walking down the street holding hands, but then he notices another woman and runs you into a parking meter, how do you show anger rather than boil over silently?

> • If you catch him in a lie and it cuts you like a knife, how do you honestly express your loss of trust, rather than write him off and pretend to "be cool?"

To keep your heart from closing, you must be willing to express your heart fully and openly, without censor. Otherwise, your only option is to withdraw. In later sections, we will go into great detail about exactly how to find this level of unleashed, wild expression without repelling him. For now, just remember that the only way to stay in the present moment fully is to be in the present moment fully in every aspect of your being—physical, emotional and spiritual.

Many of us have good reasons for denying our full expression. Maybe we were punished as a child for being unpleasant. Maybe we had a man tell us we were "too much" and leave.

What stops you from being fully unleashed, and showing your authentic heart in the right-now moment?

Write down what you notice.

As it is, meeting the moment can be challenging, but when you add past hurts, it becomes even harder. When deep wounds have been inflicted, our defense mechanisms create all sorts of clever ways to prevent us from being hurt again. They do this by cutting off feeling, taking us out of the present moment. If you don't feel, you don't hurt. But if you don't feel, you don't experience love either. Love may be staring you in the face, but you are unable to receive it because you have unintentionally desensitized yourself to your surroundings.

Imagine if someone was about to punch you in the gut. Would you keep your belly soft and exposed? No. You would tense your stomach and contract your body to guard against the blow. This is what we do emotionally all the time, without realizing we are doing it. These defenses subtly distance us from experiencing the intimacy we crave. The older the defense, the more unconscious the contraction.

We may be shutting our beloved out by guarding our heart, tightening our body or limiting our breath. We could be looking straight at them, but part of us has withdrawn on a subtle level, defending against a potential hurt. In other words, even when the moment is completely safe, we are behaving as if it's not. Our childhood wound leads us to believe that if we soften into feeling, we will get hurt. So we don't soften. We repel the love that is coming toward us, then wonder where it went. We miss the moment and then wonder why we aren't loved.

Loving in full presence can sometimes feel like unwinding years of habitual closure. People start this practice and immediately become aware of all the ways they avoid the moment. For example, your man could be meeting you fully, but you notice you cannot receive his love. Your bodies may be touching, but your heart is closed and withdrawn because you don't want to risk getting hurt. The moment is as perfect as it gets, but you are unable to enjoy it. You are stuck in the past preventing yourself from opening in the now.

Love Conflict #2: Lisa Sabotages Her Relationship

Lisa had a tough childhood. Her father and mother were abusive. She learned to brace herself at all times for trouble and trust no one. Despite this, she attracted an incredible man, Brad, into her life. Brad was everything Lisa wanted in a man—attentive, supportive and trustworthy. He treated her like the most beautiful woman he had ever met, even though Lisa had always felt unattractive to other men. When he told her he would be loyal, he delivered. When Lisa was having a bad day, he was there for her. Brad was her rock.

But even though Brad was offering Lisa the deepest experience of love she had ever known, she found herself sabotaging the connection at every turn, starting fights, distancing and acting out. When Brad would tell Lisa she was gorgeous, she would say he was wrong or "just saying that." When Brad would reach out to give her a hug, Lisa would push him away. Brad was hanging in there, but Lisa could feel she was destroying the relationship. It came to a head at a wedding they attended where Lisa had a few too many glasses of champagne and spent the whole night flirting with one of the groomsmen, an unconscious ruse to test Brad's love for her. The next day, she woke up mortified at her behavior and tried to apologize, but Brad turned away and barely looked at her for hours. Lisa knew she was pushing the whole thing way too far. She didn't want to keep sabotaging their relationship, but she had no idea how to stop.

Love Solution #2: Make the Decision to Open

With coaching, Lisa was able to see she would sabotage because she had no idea how to receive the depth of love Brad was offering. Her fear of getting hurt was so great, hardwired from her past, that she found it easier to push him away than face the risk of being hurt.

In our work together, she gradually learned to soften her defenses and receive his presence, despite the sting of her childhood wounds. She learned her fears about intimacy were an artifact of the past, no longer serving her. She stopped listening to them and learned to open through them.

Now when Lisa feels Brad giving her his full attention, she ignores the protestations of her mind and instead uses her body to meet him fully. She softens the front surface of her belly, takes a full breath, feels her feet on the floor and connects to the pleasure of the moment. Embodiment gave her the tool to overcome her limiting patterns. Her past might always haunt her, but today she has a new choice. Rather than close, she has the choice to land in the present moment, open and let love in. The need to sabotage was replaced by the practice of embodied love.

If you find yourself in moments like Lisa where you are sabotaging against your will, recognize this is quite common. It's a defense mechanism which unintentionally repels love.

When traumatized by old hurts, many women cannot release their vigilance. They fear getting so lost in someone else that they lose all sense of self. They fear feeling so devoted to another that they cannot bear to live without them. They fear the very thing their deepest heart craves: full surrender into ecstatic love.

There is nothing to fix about this but to make the decision to open into the moment, feel your vulnerability and show up to love. Recognize the defense mechanism that served your survival in childhood may no longer be serving your deepest expression of love in adulthood. In fact, it's destroying your chances of deep love.

You have two choices in every moment—continue to hold back out of fear or un-guard your heart and meet the right-now moment fully. If you choose to hide yourself, you attract others who hide as well. If you choose to meet the moment fearlessly as love, you attract a partner who is unafraid to meet the moment fully as consciousness.

Through His Eyes: Why I Love Her Full Expression, Even When It's Unpleasant, by Justin

A deep man wants to grow. A deep man is inspired by challenge, not shut down by it. Inspire him with the expression of the full force of your love, and your rightful man will meet you there, and those who can't handle it will be conveniently steered away.

I'm not going to sugarcoat it: a woman's unguarded heart is vast, complex and, at times, quite terrifying. But it's invaluable to a conscious man.

When Londin shows me her raw emotions, without any filter, they have the power to snap me out of unconsciousness and draw me back into full presence. It is from here my clarity is restored. Her authentic heart will always show me exactly where I stand in relationship to her and my purpose.

The wisdom of Londin's heart empowers me to know how I need to adjust to show up to the moment as the man I am at my core. Through her willingness to land in the right-now moment, fully expressed with me, Londin reflects when I am unconscious, untrustworthy and off course.

That said, it's never easy to receive a woman's storm. It's excruciating to feel a woman's heart close, body shut down, and emotions distance themselves. Even the deepest men will struggle at times. However, any man who has experienced a fully loaded woman knows it is far more painful to suffer the alternative: harbored resentment.

If you withhold your true feelings when he goes unconscious and says or does something that hurts you, he will have no idea why you are upset. All he will see is things were fine a moment ago and, for some mysterious reason, now they're not. You will feel like a game he cannot win. Frustrated, he will find it easier to ignore you, leave the room or go out with the boys. Both of you are left feeling hurt.

What every man needs is for his woman to show him how he is making her feel in the exact moment, whether he is making her feel ecstatic pleasure or crushing pain.

Keep in mind, showing him how you feel is very different than telling him how you feel, or lecturing him or berating him for the ways he has failed you. Your expression must come from your heart, not your mind. He can debate your story, and he often will, but he can never deny the truth of your heart. Shown artfully, your raw emotion is the most transformative and seductive thing there is.

*** *Breathe* ***

6

Three Steps to Meeting the Moment

Presence is a state of being. It exists when your awareness is undivided, when the full force of your being is engaged with your partner in the right-now moment, with no distractions and nothing held back.

Have you ever felt a moment with your lover when the whole world disappeared and there was nothing but the two of you?

This is what it feels like to be totally present in sacred intimacy. Usually, people think this level of passion is only possible in the first few months of a relationship. Actually, you can have this for a lifetime if you are willing to do the work.

There are three steps to creating a state of presence when you are with your lover:
1. Let Go of the Past
2. Release the Future
3. Meet the Moment

Step 1. Let Go of the Past
The first step is to set aside the past, completely and totally. This includes both the distant and recent past: what he or you did today, last week, last year, last decade.

You will know you have fully released all aspects of the past if you can gaze into your partner's eyes as if you just met. If you just met him, you would carry no stories or preconceived notions. You would take him in without bias, pay attention to how he makes you feel, and respond directly and only to those feelings.

You know you are not there if you tighten up because all you can think about is something he did to piss you off, lose your trust or let you down in the past, whether that past was five minutes ago or five months. While those hurts do live in your body and affect the now, they aren't an excuse to close down. Closure is whatever you do with your body to pull away, quit playing, shut him out and stop the flow of love.

When the hurts bubble up, the practice is to take a deep breath, open your heart, soften your body and display how you are feeling—sad to happy, fierce to tender, angry to ecstatic. When you show him how you feel from a softened body, you invite him into you rather than push him away. To do anything else is to hold back love and deny him the full force of your loving presence.

Step 2. Release the Future
The second step to achieving presence in intimacy is to release any projections into the future.

You know you are projecting into the future if you find yourself thinking, "I'm getting too deep, he could hurt me. Time to put on the brakes." Maybe he's bringing you amazing presence and it makes you feel so good, it actually causes you concern. If you lost him, you could never get over the heartache of not having this presence in your life. Here's the thing: if you put on the brakes, you put a limit on intimacy. You literally squeeze off your ability to feel met by him, and you push him away simultaneously.

Can you imagine that? Some of us spend our whole lives hoping for a fairy tale romance—and when it presents itself, we push it away to avoid getting hurt. We tell ourselves that we need more time, reassurance or proof, and then we'll open. The problem is there's never enough time, reassurance or proof. At one point, we must stop making excuses to justify withholding love.

Intimate surrender is a choice. When we choose to allow the fullness of the moment, open heart and soft body, we choose surrender. With total surrender, we get what we desire—the full flow of love.

Many clients express trembling fear about being rejected yet again, or hurt the same way they were time and time before. Remember, you create that hurt if you close yourself off. If you shut down to him, you drive him away. The only choice is to open and give it all you've got.

At some point, you just need to trust in the goodness of your divine plan and stop trying to control it. You cannot desire to love with abandon and at the same time play it safe. To project into the future is to play it safe.

Step 3. Meet the Moment
When your man turns to you and offers you his undivided attention, can you receive it? Can you shift out of your mind enough that you can let his attention in? Can you meet the moment fully?

I call this level of presence the "Super Bowl moment." In American football, the Super Bowl is the biggest and most important game of the year. All the practices and plays come together in a game that means everything, and everyone gives it their all. In intimacy, the Super Bowl moment is when you have your man's full and complete presence, and it's time to bring all you've got for the deepest loving possible.

A good example of this is when he tells you to pack your bags—he's taking you away. He sets work aside, turns off his phone, places you in some super romantic atmosphere and looks into your eyes. In that instance, do you meet his gaze right back or do you suddenly feel antsy, notice you don't like his shirt or stress out that your dress is ugly and your hair doesn't look right?

It's amazing what shows up in us when the Super Bowl moment arrives. Our clients laugh with us about this all the time. You would think it would be bliss. Instead, we see that it's too intense and the fear of getting hurt sends alarm bells sounding through our bodies. We have endless ways to reduce the intensity, including complaining, starting a fight, checking our phone or even wondering if the partner we've been desiring forever is actually the "one."

All of these behaviors represent a way to stay safe and unloved. If a Super Bowl moment comes and we push it away, it is we who are keeping love at bay. We realize we cannot meet the moment. The lack of deep intimacy in our lives is no one's fault but our own. We recognize that part of practice is to learn how to let love in when it comes.

Nobody Said Presence Was About Being Quiet or Subdued

By now you are seeing we are not just talking about sitting in Buddha-like stillness or transcending emotion when we say presence. The awakened woman's version of presence looks more like the grand displays of nature fully unleashed. We are talking about living in your fullness in the now.

A great example of this is the stereotypical hot-blooded Latina woman. She feels, she emotes. She experiences, she responds. There is never a shadow of a doubt of what is happening within her, as it is revealed a thousand times in her expression. Rather than holding back, hiding or pretending, she allows for an uncensored exchange to occur between herself and her man. She is not controlling the moment, she is the moment. It is as mesmerizing as a summer lightning storm, natural power displaying its majesty. Most notably, it is a supreme reflection of the energetic truth of the moment, which gives her man the opportunity to step up. That is where the value in fullness lies—the piercing truth of the heart, fully revealed, as a gift to awaken the world.

For any fully embodied emotional display to serve, it must be coming from an open heart as a true, authentic reflection of the right-now moment. Just because a person is free-flowing in their emotion does not mean they have an open heart. If you are wagging your finger at your partner, shaming or blaming him, or saying things like, "You always do this," or "You never do that," you are not in the right-now moment. Your fullness is based in past stories, resentments and closures. This isn't openness, it's a tantrum. You will incite him into equal and opposite closure, take away his confidence and steer him into collapse. Most importantly, you do not serve his awakening. He could apologize, and that is nice, but that is a therapy moment, a meeting of the minds. If you want to awaken ravishing presence from him, you need to be in the body, in the right-now.

For anyone who has difficulty expressing emotions, it's important to work on vocalizing your felt experience. For those who are already highly expressive, cultivate the ability to express love with an open heart in the right-now moment.

7

How the Love-Driven Being Shows Up to Love: Three Asanas

To help you begin finding this level of totally spontaneous authentic expression, we want to give you some concrete practices. The asanas and assignment you will read in this chapter are designed to train your body-mind to liberate your uncensored essence.

As we saw already, to feel met in a relationship, we need to be able to let go of the past, release the future and meet the moment fully.

We saw how the untrained mind obsesses upon the past and the future and how that takes you out of the moment. A powerful way to land deeper in the moment, then, is to get out of the mind and drop into the body. This is where you bring in the yoga. When you put all the attention on the yoga, the yoga brings you into a deeper experience of the right-now moment.

Here are three foundational asanas from the Yoga of Intimacy™ to help you stay juicy in your body and tenderized in your expression.

1. Allow Breath - The thing about breath is that it helps you feel your full self. So when you freeze and go into defense, the first thing your body will do is restrict breath. Shallow breathing will diminish the radiance you have to offer him—all of your juiciness and fullness. It will turn you into a shell of yourself.

When you allow the deepest parts of your belly to fill with breath, you will invite more feeling into your body and increase your energy. It will feel as if you are inhaling beauty, juiciness and vitality. Breath is life. You literally become more beautiful when you're breathing fully because you are enlivened. Even if what you are feeling isn't pleasant, the breath will always help you feel more alive and present.

In the beginning of this book, we described how to breathe fully down the front surface of your body. Now, considering what you just read, let's practice another breath. This is the exact breath you will take when you feel yourself getting stuck, frozen or holding back your authentic heart when relating to your lover.

*** *Breathe* ***

2. Soften the Body - Remember when we described someone preparing to punch you in the gut, how you noticed you would tense up so you didn't feel the blow? A lot of us walk around our entire lives tensed up so we don't have to feel the perpetual blows which occur all day every day.

This is kryptonite to sacred relating. Sacred relating is about savoring every nuance. To do that, we need to soften and surrender the front surface of our body so we can feel again. One way to do this is by noticing where you are holding tension and relaxing the muscles in that area. A lot of the women I work with say, "I feel so numb." Well, numbness comes from defense. Numbness comes from not breathing and not softening. If you breathe and soften, you're going to experience a tidal wave of feeling. And this fully-feeling you is what attracts him and inspires him to show up in depth.

3. Find Flow - Once breath is restored, and you've let down the defenses, feelings will come. In this asana, you allow your body to display the authentic flow of your emotional truth. You become fully responsive—a living reflection of the truth of the field between you and your partner. This only works if it's coming from your authentic heart. It's not a gift if it's coming from motive, manipulation or closure. When it's true and full, it will feel vulnerable, exposed and possibly crazy, but to your partner it is an invitation to dive right into you.

There's nothing more erotic for a man than being able to feel the effect of his presence on you. And ultimately, from the point of view of giving, this is your gift. As you heard from Justin, a deep man gets into a relationship with a full woman so that he can see the truth of his consciousness reflected through her heart. She becomes his Oracle. When he goes unconscious, she shows him her hurt. When he collapses, she shows him her frustration. When he falls off course, she shows him her distrust. She shows him as love, from love, because she loves him.

You don't have to be bulletproof. You don't have to be badass. You don't have to meet him in the stillness of consciousness. You get to be all of life and just express. That's very different than relating unconsciously, and filling the silence with nervous chatter because we can't take the intensity of the moment (i.e., spitting off energy to avoid feeling). We're not expressing from the mind, we're expressing from the body.

If your current or future man were sitting with you now, could you receive his penetrative gaze? How do you hold your body to let his presence into you? The three asanas give you the keys to becoming permeable enough that you invite your man to dive into you. That's where you capture his heart and enrapture his being. Show him your heart. Unguard it. Undefend it, and reveal its exact authentic state. Nothing to pretend and nothing to dumb down. You don't have to be anything other than you.

If you're a total goofball, playfully be the dork that you are. If you get lost and feel awkward, tell him you don't know what to say. If he does something that repulses you, show him your disgust. If he brings you pleasure, show him your pleasure. This is true whether you're dating or it's your long-term partner. When you're in a relationship and he finally gives you that Super Bowl moment, can you receive it? Can you let go of your disappointment of all the times he didn't, and let his right-now presence ripple across your soft, surrendered, feeling body?

If you let an open body lead the way, you will naturally bring wisdom. The antics of the mind mean little if you stay connected to the body. Your anxiety may be peaking, but it is what you do with your body that impacts him most.

It is how we conduct love which inspires our partner to meet us in the right-now moment...or not.

This is why we practice intimacy as a yoga. Our defense mechanisms invite us to shut down, play it safe, push him away. The yoga invites us to open anyway. It is not always comfortable to open, but it has a profound effect on intimacy.

- When fear bubbles up, warning you to rein in your desire, you soften your heart instead, relax the belly and take a deep breath. He feels the vulnerable invitation of your body and dives into your heart with the presence of his conscious love.

- When insecurity rolls in, making you want to hide your body or turn away, you soften instead, meet his gaze and courageously let him see your vulnerability. He feels your tender heart and is inspired to step into you with depth.

- When he does something to lose your trust and you feel the urge to shut down, you unleash your storm, displaying your sadness or anger as a gift to awaken his integrity. He feels the truth that he lost consciousness and at the same time, your invitation for him to re-gain consciousness, and thus he takes the chance to course-correct and earn your trust again.

To shut down is to end possibility. To stay present is to invite deeper intimacy. Presence is a skill. The more you cultivate it, the better you get.

This is the yoga: in order to let love in, we must let all past and future go; and all it takes is for us to open and meet the moment fully.

The "Yes" Practice

You can practice deepening your relationship to love now, without a partner. It starts with feeling the flow of love through your own body. It's not uncommon for women to feel numb and disconnected from their bodies. This can be a function of having experienced abuse and developing a pattern of disassociating from the body. Or it can be a sad outcome to sitting in front of a computer all day. Or you may just want more pleasure running through your love making.

To feel more pleasure coursing through your body, we suggest doing what we call the "Yes" Practice. You can do the "Yes" Practice formally or you can do it casually throughout your day. Let's start with the casual version of the "Yes" Practice.

The Casual "Yes" Practice

What this involves is becoming aware of your body, bringing attention to your felt experience in the moment and looking for any pleasurable sensation which feels like a "yes" to you. For example, your chest might feel tight and constricted, but is there some simple pleasure to a stretch of your spine in this moment? If so, stretch your spine and say "yes" to that pleasure. Whisper "yes" out loud to yourself.

This may feel funny at first. And that's okay. We do a lot of really funny things—but they work. As you keep going, place your attention on the felt experience of the moment and specifically keep finding sensations in your body that feel good. No matter what else is going on, focus on something—any one thing—that feels wonderful about your body. It could be the breeze on your skin, a stretch of your neck or a deep, cleansing breath.

Find any one thing right now.

Just in this short moment, were you able to feel even the slightest hint of pleasure moving through your body? If yes, however large or small, that's perfect. If no, that's okay. Notice if judgment comes up for you—or fears or excuses. Rather than giving them authority, discipline your mind to embrace your body and shower it with love. Many of us have been conditioned to spend most of our time focusing on the negative feelings which are circulating in our bodies or on cravings for food or incessant troubling thoughts of a broken love relationship. This leads to a relationship with the body which can feel like a battleground. The "Yes" practice rewrites that relationship toward pleasure.

These things take time and they will come with practice. Just continue to explore your body and breath until you find a specific movement or area that does feel pleasurable and when you find it, say, "yes." Some of you may find it within seconds, others within minutes, hours or even months. Trust the process and you will improve greatly with practice.

You can do this sitting at your desk in the middle of a hectic work day to breathe some life back into your body. You can do it on a short walk outside in nature. Even a few seconds of this practice can do wonders for keeping pleasure and embodiment in the picture. If you'd like to take this practice a step deeper, you can do it in a more formal way.

The Formal "Yes" Practice

To go deeper with this, you will want to find a private space where you can relax, and feel comfortable closing your eyes and making noise. You will set a timer to keep your attention directed for a specific amount of time. We recommend to start with ten minutes and increase as you get more adept at this.

You can do this practice while reading along for the first couple of times or we've created a guided audio download for you which will allow you to simply close your eyes and be taken on a journey without worrying about holding the structure of the practice.* If you choose to read along, set your timer to 10 minutes now.

Adjust the position of your body however you need to so that your body feels most open and relaxed.

Now bring your attention to your toes. What are your feet doing? Begin to feel every inch of your feet fully. Even permit your toes to curl and stretch…slowly. As you focus on the "yes" of the toes, how does that impact your breath?

From here, take a long, slow, deep breath down the front surface of your body and notice what you feel.

Once again, feel into your body: your toes, your fingers, your thighs. What needs to move? What needs to soften? What needs to adjust so this moment would become even slightly more pleasurable for you?

As you adjust, bring your attention back to your breath, and slowly inhale through your nose as you soften the back of your tongue, and invite that deep, slow breath down your throat and into your womb.

Take your time. Give yourself a minute or two to really find it. Can you find a pleasure point? Where is it? Locate it now.

Once you find that pleasure point, whether it be in your toes, between your thighs or in the center of your heart, say "yes" to the sensation. By saying "yes" out loud, you stimulate your vocal chords, creating greater openings. You also reassure the inner child that it is okay to feel pleasure. If you find yourself too shy to speak it out loud, you can say "yes" in your mind. But just know, your ultimate goal is to be able to confidently bring volume to your sensation.

Continue softening into your pleasure point. Notice, is it moving to a different area? Is the area getting more sensitive or less? Whatever happens is fine, just continue to stay with it, and remember…breathe.

Every few seconds, sound another "yes." Imagine your "yes" dilating, amplifying the feeling, making it larger and ever more lush. And with every inhale, receive the pleasure of it fully with another "yesss."

Now, we invite you to close your eyes and immerse yourself in the exploration until time runs out, and then turn to the next page.

Welcome back.

Notice if you're eager to drop the practice and climb back into the comfort of your head space. Or maybe it's the opposite, and you're still still basking in the goo of pleasure and find it hard to transition out. There's no right or wrong—just mindful observations.

Now that you're back, on a scale from 0-10, how much pleasure were you able to find? 0 being you found no pleasure at all, and 10 being you were fully immersed in ecstasy.

Write that number here: _____

If you gave yourself a 6 or below, what was blocking you from receiving the pleasure of the moment? Was it thoughts of judgment or unworthiness? Was it physical pain? Was it emotional pain? Was it a busy mind?

If you gave yourself a 7 or above, what's one way you could creatively bring this practice to your next intimate encounter?

Write down your answers.

_____

_____

_____

_____

_____

_____

_____

Whatever number you gave yourself this time, do not judge it. Let it be a motivating reflection of your current relationship to your own pleasure, and possibly explain some of the results you may be experiencing in the bedroom.

This is a powerful practice to reveal your current relationship to pleasure. And remember, the amount of pleasure you can feel on your own is directly correlated to the amount of pleasure you will be able to feel with a partner.

In the intimate occasion, it is the pleasure that you experience in your own body that quite literally attracts and draws out the full force of your lover's presence. If you are withholding, or unable to access the pleasure of your own essence (your love-body), your partner will likely match you, reciprocally, in withholding or be unable to access his full presence.

To live a life where we are fully met by love, we need to do our part and that is to cultivate our ability to receive the full force of our own essence, as love. We do this by returning to the "Yes" Practice regularly. We do this through allowing breath, softening our defenses, unleashing authentic expression, and being willing to say a full-bodied "yes" to the good stuff.

***If you'd like to experience Londin
leading you in The "Yes" Practice, go to
www.AwakenedWomansGuide.com/resources
to find a free guided audio practice.**

8

The "Historical No"

Sometimes we want to be a "yes," but we can't seem to let it happen. We trust the man and the moment and we want to open with all of our heart and body, but we find ourselves stuck in a "no" beyond our control. We find ourselves completely blocked, locked out from love and buried in our fears.

When this happens, we are dealing with a "historical no." A historical no is a no which comes from the past and has absolutely nothing to do with the present. It is a defense mechanism we set up at an earlier time in our life, when we felt we needed it. Maybe our brother chronically abused us, so we learned to shut down our body to avoid inviting his advances. Maybe our first boyfriend cheated on us and we vowed to never relax into love again.

The problem with a historical no is it goes on auto-repeat, creating distrust in all the wrong moments. In other words, we might be in the presence of a trustworthy man who is treating us like a queen, but we cannot relax no matter how hard we try. We are stuck, bracing ourselves for impact, waiting for the other shoe to drop, even though he has given us no reason to distrust him. Either we pick a fight, look down at our phone, get antsy or simply go numb. Once the dust settles and we've pushed our partner a million miles away from us, we stand in the wreckage and ask ourselves, "Why the hell did I do that?"

When we do this, we actively block out the love we are being given. We cannot fully receive it. Sadly, our men will do one of two things when we do this. They will either give up and move on to someone who can receive what they offer. Or, they will stay with us, but stop giving love because it's not being received, and the relationship will skid into mediocrity.

It's depressing to find yourself in a juicy moment with your man, getting his full attention, and notice yourself unable to meet him there. The "historical no" is very tricky, but there is a way out. Let's look at a real-life example.

Love Conflict #3: Emily Repels Mr. Right

Emily's new love interest Tom texts her to be ready at 7:00 p.m. He is taking her on a surprise date! Emily is elated because Tom is the best guy she has met in years.

The date starts out perfect. Tom brings her flowers, opens the car door for her and then takes her to a chic restaurant she's been wanting to try for years. Emily can't believe it—it's like Tom knows exactly what she wants before she even tells him.

And that's the problem. With each heroic move on Tom's part, Emily gets a little more uncomfortable. It's never been this good before. She doesn't know what to do. Her heart starts racing. She starts obsessing in her mind whether she's good enough for Tom, whether he's expecting sex in return for his kindness and whether this is all too good to be true. She cannot receive what he's giving. She cannot land in the moment of it all. The perfect date is now causing her tremendous anxiety and going downhill fast.

Emily starts acting distant. Tom wonders what he did wrong. Inside she's thinking, "Why the hell am I acting like this?!" and Tom is thinking, "Why did I bother?"

By the end of the date, everything feels awkward between them. Tom gives her a weak hug, jumps in his car and doesn't look back. Emily texts him several times over the next few days, but he doesn't answer. Crushed, the next weekend Emily goes back to the bad boy at the bar, Bobby, who behaves like a douche. Ironically, Bobby is more comfortable for her because he's already a let-down. He represents an easier scenario than Tom—no pressure, no risk.

Love Solution #3: Unwind Your "Historical No"
The real tragedy here is that Emily didn't mean to repel Tom. Sadly, it was as if she couldn't help herself, like she didn't have a choice.

We helped Emily understand she was dealing with a "historical no." We had her look into her earlier relationships with men— dad, brother, cousins, early boyfriends. When she did, she realized she had been sexually abused and felt victimized by the men closest to her. She had learned not to trust love because "love" hurt her horribly in her formative years. She actually felt more comfortable around untrustworthy men like Bobby because they matched what she was expecting to receive—abuse.

We worked with Emily in two ways. First, we had her do the daily "Yes Practice" with herself to reclaim her own sexual flow. She had to learn how to embrace positive sexual energy, first in the safest of ways—by herself.

Then we worked on helping her embrace positive sexual energy from a man. We worked intensely with her on how to relax and receive a man's energy when she felt it was able to be trusted in the present moment. We had her practice with a surrogate partner where a man would give her perfect presence without approaching or touching her, clothes on. This gave her a safe environment in which to re-train the responses in her body. In the same way you would learn to walk after an accident, step-by-step training the body to move in a certain way, Emily practiced very slowly and deliberately to breathe, relax and open her body in the presence of a man she could trust.

In the beginning, she would have panic attacks. Even though the moment was a practice scenario, she was with a trusted surrogate, and no actual sex or touching was involved, she would still go into the automatic "no." The fear of violation was so intense, so imprinted from her past. She faced it again and again, overcoming the old conditioning and learning a new way. Over time, together in sacred practice, we created new pathways in her nervous system where she could land, not in the past, but in the right-now moment and, from that place, let love in. We helped her create a second option that had nothing to do with the "historical no." We helped her create the ability to receive quality love.

Today she is in a thriving relationship with one of the "good" guys and she is thrilled to be past the auto-closures of her childhood, carving a new path of experience and presence with each day that passes.

If you find yourself pulling an Emily here, realize this is old programming in your body. It might even be unconscious for you. In other words: depth shows up; you are unable to receive it, so you push it away without meaning to, and then wonder why your love life lacks depth. This is the case for so many women we see who cannot seem to find a good man no matter what they do. They find out through our work that they are repelling the good men before they even register the men have arrived.

When you are dealing with a "historical no," you need to do work to actively create a new response other than the auto-response from the past. You do this first by yourself, learning to receive pleasure on your own. The "Yes" Practice is incredible for this and so simple. Then you need to do work to learn to receive the efforts of a man you can trust. The best way to do this is to put yourself in front of conscious men and practice receiving what they are giving. This is the kind of thing you would do in a workshop or private session. Both of these will teach you how to land in the right-now moment and receive the goodness that comes your way.

Now, not every inadvertent closure is a historical no. If you occasionally find yourself being a "no" when you really wish you could be a "yes," that's not a big deal—it sucks, but it's not a pattern. If you find yourself doing it so often that it ruins your relationships and leaves you alone and sad, that's when you know you are stuck in a closed loop. It's like your childhood wounds have constructed a revolving door of reality you cannot seem to exit. It is ironic because the defenses were designed to protect you, but now only serve to block your best interests.

It becomes a self-fulfilling prophecy. In the fear of getting hurt, you brace for impact and reduce your love-flow. Your partner feels the diminishment and pulls back as well. Suddenly, you just created the exact thing you didn't want to have happen.

Closure is a relational pattern designed with one goal in mind—to keep us safe. While the pattern may be incredibly isolating and lonely, it is far less scary than venturing into the unknown, which could lead to violation, rejection or being shamed. No matter how terrible the "historical no" feels, it is familiar, safe and, to the inner child, preferable to taking risks.

Making the decision to open in the right-now moment is the game-changer. It will change your life and relationships forever, especially if you do it impeccably and without compromise. It's not easy. You will confront the fear of the unknown, the anguish of your past, and the terror of potentially facing rejection, hurt and pain. You may feel pathetic in your vulnerable display, wishing instead to be one of those women who is bulletproof and hardened. But, you will be able to embrace newness. And newness keeps love thriving.

Keep in mind, it is not always a good decision to open just for anyone, anywhere. You can and should always be open with people you trust, but sometimes closing to another is appropriate. Namely, it's helpful to do when you most certainly do not want intimacy.

For example:

- Maybe a creep has approached you and you feel a very definitive no.
- Maybe a man has violated your trust so intensely you have decided he's out and it's time to kick him to the curb.
- Maybe a man you've been dating advances on you too quickly and you're a clear no.

All of these times are examples of appropriate moments to stop the flow of energy between yourself and another. Openness is not black and white. It is a living, breathing choice informed by the wisdom of the heart and body.

When we stand in the unknown, and allow the moment to reveal what is next, we invite spontaneity and transcend habit. It doesn't matter if we've been together for a decade. We can experience the invigoration of a brand-new fresh moment whenever we land in the now, in presence. If we can achieve that with our beloved, we have an infinite variety of notes to choose from in our symphony together.

Imagine two pianists coming together with every single note available at each of their fingertips. There's no limit to the music they can create.

*** *Breathe* ***

Through His Eyes: Repelling or Inspiring His Presence, by Justin

A man wants you to be bubbling over with love's flow, showering him in sensuality and delight. Every time he offers his loving presence in just the right way, he needs you to receive and respond hugely in order for him to ever be willing to do it again. Otherwise, work, TV, beer and doing nothing sound a whole lot better.

Left to his own devices, a man will gravitate toward laziness, unconsciousness and doing nothing as often as possible—or work like hell to achieve that level of freedom in his life. While these activities might sound a little slovenly, they are his way of taking a break from life's endless laundry list of to-dos. It's his way of nourishing himself and recharging his battery before the next momentous shitstorm of tasks enters the picture. To keep this man present after a long day requires something more interesting than food, beer, television and sleep. Most women have no idea that presence requires a great deal of effort on a man's part. He will only offer it if it has an effect.

What does a man need for him to straighten his spine, breathe deeply into his core and give you his unshakeable presence? He needs you to receive his presence and show him the effect it has on you.

To help you practice this, the three beginning asanas of the Yoga of Intimacy™ are an excellent place to start: allow your breath, soften your body and find your authentic flow. To feel a woman totally responsive, soft and authentic is like a breath of fresh air for a man. He requires your vulnerable, fierce transparency to motivate, and that you continue to show up inspired. Otherwise, he has no idea of how his presence impacts you, and figures it has no impact at all. Therefore, it isn't worth giving.

Guide your man to become the ideal lover by receiving his presence when he's giving it, even if it doesn't feel like it's enough. When your man offers you his attention, touch, clarity or strength, respond 10 times more than you think is normal. Remember, most men have denser bodies than women, and therefore less sensitivity, so when you show him your pleasure or pain, do so even more enthusiastically or overtly than you think you need to do.

Quite literally, he wants to feel your body like an ocean, responding to his every gesture, in those moments when he offers his full attention or looks into your eyes or touches you just the right way. This is a sure way to inspire him to do it more.

9

Everyday Blocks to Presence
(And How to Avoid Them)

W hat you may be seeing by now is how you are either degrading the moment or deepening it with how you show up. It is your ability to feel your body and let your mind release which will determine how deeply you meet your partner in presence.

When we meet our partners in intimacy, we are meeting them body to body. It doesn't matter how much we know or understand about relational dynamics; it's the quality of our embodiment that matters most. If we cannot land in our bodies, we simply cannot deepen in intimacy with another. It will always feel mind-to-mind, surface and shallow, stuck in the past, fearful of the future or relating at a safe, yet lonely distance.

Let's look at some of the most common blocks to presence in relationships:

1. Getting Stuck in the Mind

There is an epidemic of people struggling to feel deep, authentic connection. We are a digital culture. Between computers, smart phones, televisions and so on, we spend almost all of our time ignoring the body and engaging the mind. We sit all day, from the desk to the car to the couch. Seldom do we actively practice relating body to body from presence.

When we find ourselves wanting intimacy with our partner, suddenly our body plays an important role, not just in the sexual occasion, but anytime we are in the same room with them. Whether we are aware of it or not, our posture, breath and movements have an effect. They are either turning our partner on or turning them off.

After hours of relating to the world mind to mind, how do we possibly feel past our necks and drop into the embodied experience of love?

Modern life will pound away at your intimacy if you let it. It is up to you to stop the trend. You do this by taking time out of your day to get into your body. You put the rat race aside for a time, and drop into practice. We outlined three asanas of the Yoga of Intimacy™. What if you regularly set aside 30 minutes to cultivate these three asanas in your body? You could do this through dance, movement, yoga, gardening, cooking or anything else that brings you great joy and openness.

This is what it looks like to be a practitioner of sacred intimacy. You prioritize the body. People often think it takes meeting the perfect person to place yourself in the path of sacred relationship. In fact, it is the quality of your embodied spiritual practice that invites this level of deep, intimate loving.

2. Letting Habit Squash Spontaneity

As intimate partners spend more and more time together, they get into habits of relating. It happens in the nervous system where you are so habituated to a set of behaviors that you can perform them without even thinking about it. A great example of this is the ability to drive to and from work without thinking consciously about the path. We can navigate our long-term intimacy on autopilot as well.

When habits take over, spontaneity dies. Rather than responding artfully to the right-now moment, we relate from conditioning. Over many years, these set patterns of relating have a terrible side effect.

They reduce the number of keys available on the "piano of notes" we can play with our partner. Each habit eliminates a key until we may be playing with just three or four notes. This is where monotony sets in, such as making love the exact same way time after time even though it bores you. In the beginning, those three notes might feel darn interesting, but stay together for years and suddenly the repetitiveness of those three notes make you feel like you are dying of boredom.

Habits train us to ignore the precious potential of the present moment. The habits dull our senses and put us on autopilot not just in our intimate relationship, but in our entire life. Remember when we talked about relating to our partner as if we were meeting them for the first time? This is an example of how you can break out of habit and land yourself in the now. The practice is the key to creating newness and excitement in a long-term relationship.

3. Feeling Unworthy of Love

When someone looks deeply into your soul, you confront all of your deep-seated beliefs about your own worthiness. You see the limits to your capacity to handle large energetic flow. You face your fears around love and unconscious barriers to intimacy.

Profound love is the thing we say we want, but sometimes when it shows up, we find ourselves hiding behind a wall of fear.

> • We might be getting great adoration from him, but we go down the rabbit hole of anxiety, feeling self-conscious and unworthy of his attention, so stuck in our thoughts we can't feel his presence.

> • We might be getting his undivided attention, but suddenly feel resentful of his presence, thinking "now is good, but you don't do this enough, so you suck" and totally miss the moment.

• We might be getting the foreplay we always wished he would offer, but find ourselves numb and unable to enjoy the pleasure of his touch, our body walled off from feeling due to the nature of our lifestyle, whether it's too much caffeine, too much time on the computer or too many recreational numbing agents.

These kinds of behaviors have one root cause—we don't feel worthy of love. When we don't feel worthy of love, we unconsciously push it away. We make choices that repel the moments we spent our whole lives waiting for. The Super Bowl moment arrives and we fumble the play.

Left to our own devices, our minds will be like rats in a cage, running from one fearful thought to the next. Any form of drifting in your awareness marks an inability to meet the moment. The thoughts and fears might feel real, but they aren't. They are illusions to pull you out of the circumstances of the present.

4. Chit-Chat, Gossip and Mundane Conversation

The right-now moment is such a deep, connective space that communicating in unconscious ways can easily pull you away from it. Chatting is one of the most common intimacy killers. It usually starts happening when the moment feels too intense. How often have you been around someone who begins talking incessantly just to fill the empty space? They do it to mask how uncomfortable they feel. However, what you'll notice is they are repelling their partner and not even noticing because they are simply not present. Endless chatter defuses the energy, which makes things more comfortable for the one chattering and less fulfilling for both partners.

Most casual conversation will likely take you out of the right-now moment and place you in the past or future: "Did you hear that Jennie broke up with Bill? Did the kids score okay on the Spanish test? Are the roofers coming next week for the quote?" This is what many couples spend their time doing on a date. They let all the mundane details of life suck the juice right out of their dynamic. While a certain amount of this is necessary for running a life, and some of it is just plain fun, it's important to keep it in check when you are craving intimacy with your lover.

5. Expecting Perfection

Waiting for things to be perfect before you are willing to open yourself to your partner gives you a giant excuse to avoid receiving the moment. If you nit-pick everything your partner does or doesn't do, you get stuck in a loop of endless complaints. The problem is, he'll rarely measure up and so both of you are left with the feeling of being unmet. It's important to notice if you are using his "failure to get it exactly right" as an excuse to not receive what he is offering.

Telling yourself you would open if only he would _____ (fill in the blank) is simply another way to avoid feeling vulnerable and meeting the moment. We see this often. Let's look at an example.

Love Conflict #4: Sonya Demands Perfection

Sonya's man Charlie works internationally and has been away from home for weeks. He arrives back into town and calls her right away, telling her to get dressed, it's couple time! Sonya is thrilled.

The problem is, as soon as Sonya sees Charlie, she feels repelled by what he is wearing. When they arrive at the restaurant, she hates the place he's chosen. When he starts telling her about his trip, she's terribly annoyed he's not asking about what has been going on in her world.

Sonya's heart sinks because she has looked forward to this moment for weeks and now that it's here, everything feels all wrong. She is totally bummed out and turned off, and starts nit-picking Charlie for all of his faults. By the time they order their entrees, both of them wish Charlie was still out of town.

Love Solution #4: Embrace His Effort

Sonya could recognize that expecting Charlie to be perfect takes her completely out of the moment. It blocks her from receiving his gestures of love (calling her as soon as he arrives home, taking her out and making an effort to see her).

In this scenario, she instead begins to land herself not in Charlie's failures, but in the effort he is making. Rather than wanting his perfection, she loves his trying. It's not about her pretending to have a good time when she's not or loving a choice she hates, but lightening up about it all. The truth is, Charlie is doing his best, and his heart is in the right place and that is what matters. More importantly, the reason Charlie sucks at getting little things like clothes and restaurant choices right is because he's single-focused on mission. His ability to earn a handsome income makes for a pretty lush life for the two of them. Sonya remembers she could love this about him, rather than judging him for failing in the areas in which she excels.

On top of that, the deeper issue here is Sonya's inability to land in the moment in love. She used complaints to avoid receiving. With coaching, she saw how her demands for perfection were ruining her love life. Nobody could ever measure up and she would wear men out with her incessant criticisms—Charlie wasn't the first man to pull away from her hypercritical ways, or even the tenth.

When Sonya resolved to stop expecting perfection, her whole reality shifted. She found herself receiving the kind of love she had waited her entire life to experience. She began to see all the ways Charlie was going out of his way to delight her. The flow of their love improved dramatically, and she learned to lovingly tease Charlie about his mismatched outfit and less-than-impressive restaurant radar rather than criticizing him, bringing a sense of humor to these things rather than frustration.

And if Sonya's critical side ever does rear its ugly head again, Charlie has a new strategy to call her out on it. He lovingly looks her straight in the eye and says the code word we gave them. Sonya realizes what she's doing, and they both crack up.

If you find yourself pulling a Sonya here, realize that things will never feel perfect. See it as an excuse to keep yourself closed off to the moment…and open anyway. Meet his efforts to love you and receive him the best you can. This is the Super Bowl moment. It doesn't have to look perfect to be fulfilling if you know how to enjoy his effort.

Practitioners of the yoga learn to show up to their partner in presence, no matter what. When it's time for intimate relating and suddenly crazy thoughts and feelings arise to distract you from giving and receiving love, you're able to stay put and open into the moment fully.

10

The High Price of Blocking Presence

Any time we do any of these things which block presence, we pay a very high price.

First of all, it makes us feel like there is no depth in our lives. We are left feeling unmet. While we created this feeling through our inability to be present, we usually do not make the connection that we are at cause. Instead, we think presence never showed up, that there are no "good men," or that Cupid is pointing his arrow in every direction but ours. In fact, presence is the nature of being. Therefore, if we aren't experiencing it daily, we know it's because we are blocking it.

The other major cost is what it does to our intimate partner. It takes a lot of effort on anyone's part to take their attention off their mission in life and place it entirely on you. Your man will only do this if it achieves a noticeable result—i.e., he gets to enjoy the happiness he creates in you through the offering of his presence. If you cannot receive the presence he offers, he will feel it fall flat and see no point in giving it; after all, to him, you don't appear to even enjoy it. Then you may be left wondering what happened to the man who once made the effort.

It doesn't matter who you are with or what they are offering you—if you cannot open to love, you cannot receive it. In every way, you must cultivate the ability to give and receive presence if you want to feel met in love.

Love is available to you every moment of every day. You must open to love first, and when you do, your life will begin to shift around you. The more you learn to live as that love, the more you begin to resonate those around you and the moment into love. The more you open to love, the more love is capable of flowing through your body and into your life.

Through His Eyes: Loving Beyond Closure, by Justin

When both partners start loving beyond closure, the relationship evolves into a kind of love that is beyond condition, unflappable.

For example, in a moment of tension, one of the gifts a conscious man brings his woman is the ability to see her closures better than she can see them herself. If she feels trapped, overwhelmed or beaten down by them, he is there to offer his unconditional presence as the ground beneath her feet.

He does this by dropping into the moment with her, connecting eye to eye, synchronizing breath to breath, relaxing his heart, and not needing the moment to change. It's that kind of loving presence that gives her the chance to feel the difference between what she is holding onto versus the love that is staring her right in the face.

That said, there are times when a man will bring his full presence to his woman and it's simply not enough. In the midst of her sadness, anger, or despair, sometimes no amount of effort is adequate to cut through her closure. Through his eyes, it can look as if she is imprisoned inside of her own madness, spinning out wildly, unable to receive his support. It is painful for him to show up to these moments. He may do everything he can to help her through it—talk to her, read books, go to therapy, attend workshops, etc.—but if the closure continues to prove historical, there is little he can do about it. It can leave him feeling hopeless because he knows he can support her, but he cannot heal her wound for her. That is up to her.

In intimacy, some moments will be easier than others. It's how the two of you navigate these difficult times that defines your relationship. It requires patience and vulnerability for both partners to step into the truth of the moment and open no matter what. However, these are the moments that you will remember, and will draw the two of you closer. These are the moments that redefine what love is.

11

A Decision to Open and the Epic Fuck That Followed

It's hard to emphasize enough just how critical it is to open your body and soul if you want to experience the richest intimacy possible. To give you an example of this game-changing practice, here is a detailed account of a real-life moment with Justin, when my decision to open turned a potentially depressing day into an experience of epic connection. It is the decision to open in these moments that literally makes or breaks relationships.

Coming together with Justin tonight, I felt fat. A few weeks out of a tough miscarriage and about to eat a particularly filling dinner, my body felt huge. At the restaurant, I walked into the bathroom and could feel the weight and girth of my extra bloat. Brazilian music was playing and I could feel the heaviness of my form in comparison to the music. I could feel the paralyzing effect of sitting at my computer all day writing, stillness suffocating my radiant flow. I wanted to wilt, shame myself and hide. Instead, I took a breath and decided to own it. I decided to roll my shoulders back, relax my heart and judgments and fully own my size. I quite literally made a new decision: the decision that I would stop listening to my limitations and open from a place of loving presence.

As I walked back to the table, I found worth in my current state and felt the putrid negativity of my previous mindset melt away with every step. I slid into the booth with a big smile, able to meet Justin with more of my full self, having made the decision I was beautiful as I was, my energy shifting by the minute. We enjoyed a great dinner, connecting with tender kisses that made the waitress blush.

As we were walking out, Justin made a comment about me taking up the entire bed when we sleep and how much space I occupy. Immediately, I felt the urge to shrink right back into my dark hole of shame. I thought of all the other women I know who are probably much daintier than me, lighter in form and who take up much less space. I began to feel unworthy all over again. My story began to cave in on me and rob me of my power to love.

This time, rather than try to coach myself out of it, I looked at Justin with a wide-open heart and genuinely asked, "Do you love me when I take up space?" He told me he loved it—that it's one of his favorite things I do. And he meant it. Honestly, I could have never guessed that his comment could be anything other than a criticism. My story, my wound is so strong that it takes over at every opportunity. Ever since my mom chastised me I was too much and no one would ever love me, I've been buying into a story that I take up too much space and it's bad and wrong. But right now, because I questioned that story for a moment, he's telling me that my "way" delights him. Life-changing moment. I decide to let it in. Rather than dwell or argue, I receive his love. I allow it to come into my body and I relax into the joy of being loved in my fullness. The rest of the ride home, I continue to relax more and more and we drop right back into the moment with each other, basking in our date once again.

As we arrive home, Justin, feeling my surrender, continues to play with me. As I'm walking across the front yard, he grabs my ass and says, "Is this giant ass mine?" and I don't shrink at all this time. I relish the fact that my ass is huge and I say "Yes!" Then he tells me that my ass is his and he owns it and he invites me into "his" house, telling me he's going to keep me as his for the rest of his life. I've lived in this house with him for years, but I play along. He introduces me to my plants, shows me around the space, then tells me to meet him in the bedroom. When I walk in, he is lying on the bed buck naked and tells me to undress.

It's tempting at this moment to flee rather than have to stand in front of him naked. It's also tempting to put on a performance. Years of cultural programming have conditioned me to begin to think I need to create a big show, the way we see porn stars do. I can feel the thought taking me out of my body, and putting me into my head. As my attention goes to my head, I can feel the impact degrading the moment I'm sharing with Justin. I'm no longer there all the way. So, I come back into my body. I give up performance, and I offer authenticity instead. I slow down and I open. I place my hands on his chest and allow my body to melt all over him.

As a way to land fully in the now, I completely and totally soften my vaginal walls, my cervix and my hips. I give up the goal of orgasm, and instead place all of my awareness on the exact sensation that is happening and rest into it as if there was nowhere else to be but in that moment, as if that moment between us was so sufficient, it could last for an eternity. He responds to my dropping in far more than he would ever respond to me putting on a show.

We begin to meld in the most delicious merger, two bodies as one, and each moment builds organically upon the next. Every time I have an impulse to tighten, I soften. Every time I have an impulse to generate something "exciting," I relax. Every time I jump to outcome, I rest into now. And every time it gets hotter. My surrender creates something so much better than my effort ever could.

At one point, we both get taken by a current so much larger than either of us, that we spill simultaneously into wild orgasm, me screaming, him grounding, it happening individually and together until it completes on its own accord and there is nothing left but timeless stillness.

As I move to the side of him, we both lay there splayed open, deeply in love… and connected with a connection that was made possible by one decision and one decision only: the moment that started at the restaurant when I felt fat and, rather than close, I decided to open.

Summary of Pillar I: Presence

Presence is sinking into the joy of the felt, sensorial experience of the moment with your beloved.

Most of us know the feeling when we first meet someone, and we bask in what it feels like to be with them, as if time itself disappears. With presence, you can enjoy this kind of deliciousness with your beloved for a lifetime. It comes from dropping underneath the mind and bringing your body into all moments—mundane to ecstatic.

To relate sacredly is to bring your body, heart and soul to your partner in the right-now moment. The practice of presence allows you to stop telling stories from the past or projecting into the future and start living in the now. You do enough spiritual work and you realize at one point that the stories will never end. They are defense mechanisms to keep you out of the right-now moment. It is up to you to land in the moment anyway, no matter what your fearful thoughts are kicking up in any given situation.

Your body is a powerful ally to help you find presence because your body itself sits in the right-now moment. It's the mind that travels elsewhere and makes the body feel as if it's not present. Connect to what you are feeling, express it fully, and you are in the now in a powerfully, sexy way.

When we do this, we create incredible depth in relating intimately. We get to feel ourselves beyond the historical no, habits, stories, fears and closures that come fully equipped with our pasts. It is an opportunity be in the present with another for the sake of deep intimate communion.

The magic lies in showing up to the difficult moments, the ones that make you feel like you are dying. These are the places where you most avoid being present. The lure of the past is so shiny, it hooks you again and again until you insist on breaking free. You break free by showing up and letting him love you when you most want to reject his love, and by showing up and loving him when he most wants to reject your love.

Closures will always come up; no matter how many you process, there are always at least that many more to go. The thought is both beautiful and daunting because there is no end to the spiritual opening.

When you stay present in the moments that might otherwise have caused distance, the intimacy is better than ever before. That's when the lovemaking becomes explosive. It's also when you realize you deserve love in the parts of you where you didn't think it was possible. He can do that for you. You can do that for him. You lift each other up. There's nothing more beautiful than experiencing a moment where you are in the most raw, real, vulnerable place, and he holds you there; or when you hold him there, and love comes through in a way neither of you could experience without the other.

*** *Breathe* ***

Pillar I Practice: Offer a Loved One 10 Minutes of Presence

In this exercise, we invite you to pick one person (it can be a friend, a child, a parent or a lover) and offer them 10 minutes of presence today. While this practice can be done over the phone or video conference, it is best to practice in-person, body to body. This is important because it's not just your mind we want to develop in presence, but the soft, responsive tissues of your body as well.

It's also most helpful to pick someone who can meet you in the moment—in other words, someone who isn't in the middle of working, watching TV or otherwise unable to give you their attention.

Be sure to set aside all distractions (no cell phone) and, if possible, choose an environment that is appropriate for authentic connection. Keep in mind, the person you choose may not be capable of being fully present with you. This will often be the case. Your practice is not to force or demand them to be present with you, but rather, to silently invite them into presence through the quality of your practice.

Meet up with the person you've chosen and, without telling them what you are up to, offer them 10 minutes of unwavering presence through the practice described here.

1. Drop into the Right-Now Moment
Before you attempt to offer your presence to another, first you must come into presence with yourself. Begin dropping into the right-now moment by placing your attention on your own breath and your own body. To do this, try relaxing your shoulders, softening your lower belly, pressing your hands into your thighs, spreading the bottoms of your feet or slowing down your breath, inviting each inhale into the soft tissues around your heart. The key question to ask yourself is, "Where are my body and breath?" The answer should always be,

"Ah, there they are."

2. Make Eye Contact

Once you've become present with yourself, make eye contact with the loved one you've chosen. It is best to look into their left eye (the eye on the right side from your perspective) as it tends to be the more emotionally receptive side. Notice if this is difficult for you. Notice if this is difficult for them. Whether your chosen partner can meet you in eye contact or not, continue to offer them your loving gaze as a selfless gesture, as a way of showing them that you are there for them. Done skillfully, this sincere level of eye contact alone is enough to draw out tears and help move stuck emotions.

If you feel uncomfortable keeping eye contact, this is your edge of practice. Don't judge it, just notice it and keep coming back to the practice - and be sure to keep breathing as you do.

Always remember, if your gaze is locked in loving presence with your partner and you suddenly look away for whatever reason, they will feel it. And that subtle break in presence is sometimes all it takes to shift a moment of potential ecstatic union into a moment of shallow disconnection. It's like hitting the reset button and having to start from scratch. Compassionately encourage yourself to stay with them for the full 10 minutes while you lovingly invite them to meet you in depth.

3. Offer the Kind of Loving Presence They Need

As you gaze into their eye, place all of your attention on them. What's their body doing? How are they breathing? How are they feeling emotionally? Are they present or distracted?

However they are showing up, don't judge them, don't judge yourself, and don't judge the moment. There's nothing to fix here - only loving presence to be offered and an invitation for them to join you in it.

As you feel into their heart, ask yourself, "What does this person need right now to feel that they are truly loved?" Remember, what they need might be very different from what you would need. Put on the beginner's mind and assume you do not know what they need. Instead, place all of your attention on them, feel into their heart and explore the myriad ways your presence could inspire them to open in this moment.

- Maybe this person needs you to listen.
- Maybe they need a good belly laugh.
- Maybe they need your touch.
- Maybe they would be opened by watching you bubble over with joy.
- Maybe they need your undivided attention for 10 minutes.

4. Experiment, Explore, Adjust

Notice the effect you are having on your partner. Is the quality of your presence serving them? Are they opening? If not, do not fret, just continue to stay connected and subtly make an adjustment.

If you thought talking to them is what would open them most, but mid-sentence you notice it's actually closing them, it's your job to make the adjustment. Just simply pause, keep on breathing and continue offering presence to your partner as you feel into what else might serve them most - which may be just listening.

5. Receive the Moment

Let the moment move through your body as you bask in the experience of connecting with someone you love. If it sends a chill up your spine, silently say "yes" to the chill. If it cracks open your heart and you begin to shed a tear, silently say "yes" to your emotions. As you offer your loving presence to your chosen partner, you are allowing your authentic self to be seen—your heart to be a part of the equation—your truth to be the oracle of the moment. And in the midst of all this, you receive this moment by breathing it in. You must remember to breathe. Inhale the moment, breath by breath, and let it fill you, inch by inch.

Do this with your chosen partner for at least 10 minutes. If it's going well, keep going. If it's not, just commit to the 10 minutes. You can always try again, either with the same person or a different person next time. You could do this practice several times per week, or several times per day. The point is, you want to practice this skill as often as possible with those you love and trust.

The skill you are cultivating is your ability to not only meet the moment, but to become sensitive to what the moment requires to deepen in connection. This is the gift of your presence. This connection can be platonic or erotic. Either way, it is your ability to bring your yoga, presence, openness and vulnerability as a gift which serves the moment into a deeper expression of love.

Giving someone presence is harder than it sounds. Just keeping eye contact with someone for 10 minutes straight can feel foreign to most of us. If you do it right, it will feel like a stretch. At certain points the depth may begin to feel so good, it can make you nervous or start to feel awkward. This is how you know you are bumping up against your edge. This is where we suggest you spend most of your time practicing—pressed up nice and close to that edge of pleasurable discomfort. Think of presence as a muscle that can be strengthened the more you use it. And remember, your ability to give and receive presence is directly correlated to your ability to be met deeply in intimacy.

PILLAR II: POLARITY

"I think every woman wants someone to look her in the eyes, caress her cheeks and tell her to take her fucking panties off."

- Anonymous -

Introduction to the Pillar of Polarity

In Pillar I, we cultivate the ability to land in the right-now moment. In Pillar II, we hone the ability to turn on passion at will.

To land in the right-now moment with the full force of your body, mind and spirit is a skill you cultivate for a lifetime. Even the tiniest improvements have a tremendous effect on your intimate relating. But here's the catch: presence alone doesn't necessarily lead to erotic passion. Now, this is not always a problem on its own. There are countless couples happily pursuing something closer to friendship or partnership, and loving it. However, in moments where you'd like to enjoy sizzling hot sexual energy, it takes another set of skills beyond simply being present. These skills are what we explore in the Pillar of Polarity.

Polarity is important because it puts you back in control of your sex life, giving you the tools to create passion no matter how long you've been together. Even in long-term relationships, the spark doesn't have to fade over time and your desire for sex doesn't have to dry up, where chocolate becomes more interesting than cock. With polarity, your coupling can stay as bright and explosive as two Tesla coils bouncing light off each other.

Learning how to create polarity was a breath of fresh air for me. When I learned how to inspire Justin's desire any time I wanted, my life changed. I was no longer the victim to love's whimsy. This is one of the best gifts my teachers have given me. As you heard earlier, I suffered a sexless marriage where my husband deserted our bed soon after we tied the knot. Feeling that unloved, unsexy and un-fucked was beyond depressing, and left me terrified of being ignored. Polarity gave me the courage to commit again. It also gave Justin the confidence to claim me for life. For both of us, knowing we could keep the charge alive made our commitment not only possible, but thrilling.

In this section, we'll explore the following aspects of polarity:

• Why polarity is the prescription for sparking a lusterless relationship back to life.

• How you may be unintentionally turning your partner off by the way you walk, talk, breathe and move, and what to do about it.

• Why polarity has been understood exclusively through traditional gender roles, but no longer needs to be bound by them—and how you can embody a new model of relating instead.

• The three possible ways of relating in a relationship, and the pros and cons of each.

• The most important skill the modern woman can learn to simultaneously enjoy a powerful career and a rocking love life (hint: it involves exploring both sides of polarity).

• That sizzling hot moments don't "just happen" in long-term relationship, but that you can learn how to create them at any time.

• How to put it all together to create a relationship which feels loving, delicious, continually new and sexually exciting.

We'll finish by offering you a set of practices to cultivate polarity individually and with a partner to help you attract and sustain a juicy, polarized, sacred relationship.

12

Rx Polarity:
Creating a Life Filled with Sexual Excitement

At its core, polarity is a profoundly simple idea: opposites attract. It is the spark between you and another. It is the source of sexual attraction.

What it takes to sustain polarity is to understand how it works, why we fall out of it and how to generate it. Two people can deliberately ignite sizzle by understanding what drives attraction. It is physics.

Polarity works like magnets—opposites attract, sameness repels. To feel polarity, we must be in opposites. In the sexual occasion, the stronger the difference, the greater the urge to combine. In other words, if you're dying for him to kiss you, polarity is present. If you couldn't care less, polarity is missing.

Love Conflict #5: Tara Needs Dick...Bad

When Tara first met her man Dick, they were super hot for each other. They enjoyed endless sessions of amazing sex, great conversations and effortless connection. Tara was over the moon. She felt like she had met her soulmate.

However, over the course of time, the intimacy began to fade in a big way. Dick went from chasing Tara around the house to hardly noticing her. Their coffee dates went from being two people immersed in lively conversation to two people surfing their phones. Sex went from all the time to hardly ever.

By the time they came to us, they were behaving more like roommates than lovers. They got along okay. They rarely fought. But the spark was gone. If Tara scheduled a date night to rekindle the flame, the conversation would inevitably drift to the usual places—when they would fix the roof, when to invite the neighbors over, and whether Aunt Susie had lost her mind.

Tara sees other couples transfixed in each other's gaze and wonders if she will spend the rest of her life yearning for more. While she loves the stability she has with Dick, she desperately misses being ravished.

Love Solution #5: Bring Sexy Back
Tara and Dick both needed to recognize that the mundane aspects of life will beat the passion right out of their relationship. Tara and Dick did what many couples do—they chose function over fuck. They must prioritize intimacy for passion to stay in the picture.

Tara and Dick realized that life was never going to slow down. There would never be a shortage of problems or list of things to work out as a couple. Using their precious, intimate time together to talk through mundane details not only took them out of the present moment, it also chased polarity right out of the picture. To recover erotic romance, they would need to become more intentional in how they related. If they wanted their relationship to feel sexy, they needed to do the things that create sexual charge, and talking about the roof and Aunt Susie ain't it.

If you've ever felt yourself in the same position as Tara and Dick, you may be stuck in a dynamic we call resonance. Resonance is what happens when you feel like friends, business partners, or even family, but not passionate lovers. You may be getting along great, and be really productive together, but the sexual charge is nowhere to be found. While the friendship feels wonderful, the part of you that wants more than friendship eventually starts getting restless.

We are sexual beings at our core. Starved for sex long enough, we begin to crave it, like Tara—and if our relationship isn't meeting those desires, we either shut down or look elsewhere to get our needs met. People may do this in all sorts of ways, whether through watching porn, overeating, shopping, drinking, or tragically, having an affair. If you're reading this and despairing that being forever un-fucked is the price to pay for a forever relationship, do not worry. With polarity, you'll never have to make that sacrifice again.

Before we look at how to generate polarity, let's look at why we lose it. There are many reasons why a relationship can fall out of polarity. Some of the most common causes are:

1. You are in resonance but don't realize it (yet)—like Tara and Dick.
2. You realize you're in resonance but don't know how to get out of it.
3. You are unintentionally turning each other off sexually— or at least can't figure out how to turn each other on—so you both want sex but can't make it work.
4. You shut down your sex drive because you are so tired, busy or resentful of your man that you simply can't open to him sensually anymore.

We will address all of these. But remember, we won't address them from the therapeutic model. In the therapeutic approach to intimacy, we would focus on the how and why behind the dysfunction. All of the talking about our partners and analyzing the relationship gets us up in our heads. When energy is up in the head, it is most certainly not down in the genitals.

For a relationship to feel sexy, it must be approached yogically—body to body. In the yogic approach, we don't rely on analysis to re-establish intimacy. That lands us in the mind. Instead, we drop down into the body and meet the moment from breath, eye contact, sensation and the three beginning asanas of the Yoga of Intimacy™. Only meeting body-to-body, not mind to mind, guarantees hotter sex. So to allow our passion to thrive, we do the yoga. It allows us to problem-solve in a completely different way—by meeting the moment, rather than analyzing it.

This means that as we understand and practice polarity, we'll be looking at how we relate to our own body, and how that body shows up to and with our partners. Everything you do or don't do with your body, mind and spirit affects your partner. You are resonating the dynamic into friendship and/or partnership, or you are polarizing it into passion, depending upon what you bring. You are either turning your partner on or off at all times with how you walk, talk, breathe and move. So, throughout this Pillar, we will examine not just how to think about polarity, but how to embody it.

Opposites Attract

Earlier we mentioned polarity is a profoundly simple idea: opposites attract. So, what do we mean exactly by opposites?

Traditionally, sacred intimacy is taught through the lens of masculine and feminine. While it's simplest to think of masculine and feminine in terms of sex (i.e., penis equals masculine, vagina equals feminine), the truth behind these concepts reaches far beyond gender.

The 1950s represented a time when the gender-based model was in full force. Men were into masculine things. Women were into feminine things. It may not have been ideal for everyone involved, but society in general agreed upon the roles. But in today's times, that's no longer the case. Both men and women are breaking out of traditional and patriarchal limitations. We are now seeing women cultivate the skills which were once thought of as masculine: earning money, running businesses and having a strong sense of purpose. We are seeing men cultivate the qualities once thought of as feminine: nurturing others, exploring creativity and getting in touch with their feelings. As both sexes embrace these newfound freedoms, the traditional model of relationships, with strict gender roles, no longer applies. A new model is needed.

This was absolutely true for me and Justin.

Traditionally, polarity work has been taught along strict gender lines, so when Justin and I first embarked on this path, we subscribed to those teachings. We understood there was incredible wisdom to these ancient principles and we wanted to explore them thoroughly. So initially, we embraced the patriarchal extremes, with Justin playing the masculine and me playing the feminine every moment of every day. While it led to easy polarity and a lot of sexual delight, it came with a great cost. It required us to deny aspects of our full beings, to cut off or bottle up the parts of ourselves which didn't fit into that model. Not only did that limit our natural expression, but it also backfired tremendously outside the bedroom.

Both of us started to feel "off," within ourselves and with each other. My masculine side became increasingly difficult to shove down. While it was enchanting to relax and follow Justin's lead, I grew weary of never having a voice. I no longer felt willing to stay demure. I could no longer play the passive "follower" role all the time, hiding my power, swallowing my opinions and withholding my clarity. I had something to say and I wanted to say it.

Justin's feminine side, meanwhile, began acting out. While it was empowering for Justin to grow from a young adult into being a man through these practices, he became burdened doing it all the time. He grew dry, rigid and void of pleasure by constantly swallowing his emotional flow and only standing as the masculine witness. In abandoning his radiance, his spark and natural love for life dimmed. The parts we had split off were sabotaging us.

Even worse, the strict gender roles pitted us against each other, degrading our love flow. In the same way doubles partners in tennis may attack each other for losses they both contributed to, we began attacking each other for mediocre practice, blaming each other for not holding up their end of the bargain even as we struggled to maintain our own ends. We began to wonder if we were doing more harm than good and whether we should seek a deeper truth.

We soon realized we needed a bigger model in which to thrive. We spent the next three years looking into how we could maintain the benefits of polarity but modify them to avoid the extreme toll they can take on a relationship in the 21st century. It seems obvious now that we would throw out the old paradigm and replace it with a new one. But at the time, it wasn't. These gender roles are deeply ingrained in the collective unconscious and can be harder to buck than you might think.

Eventually, we felt we had no choice. We craved a model of polarity where we could let all parts of ourselves come into the picture—and we realized if we wanted to find a new paradigm, we were going to have to create it. We set out on a journey to kibosh the traditional gender roles of masculine and feminine, and to discover a new way to create polarity and build intimacy.

To move completely away from patriarchal polarity, we created a new language to define the opposing sexual poles—no longer masculine and feminine, but Alpha and Omega. It was this new language which freed us to let go of the dogma and embrace ourselves as full-spectrum beings, while still maintaining a dance of tremendous polarity. Language is powerful. It influences our thoughts and behavior in profound ways. This new language created new freedom in relating.

So, let's look at the new model.

Alpha: *traditionally considered the "masculine."*
Consciousness | Formlessness
Purpose-driven, penetrative, trustworthy—the embodiment of consciousness.
In a relationship, Alpha feels loved when trusted, and desires to penetrate their partner.

Omega: *traditionally considered the "feminine."*
Light | Form
Love-driven, receptive, radiant—the embodiment of love-light.
In a relationship, Omega feels loved when claimed, and desires to be ravished by their partner.

This language freed us because it had no judgments to it. It didn't feel sexy for me to bring Justin my "masculine" just as much as it felt unsupportive for Justin to bring me his "feminine." However, I can go into Alpha for the sake of serving our highest good and that feels super hot and sexy for both of us. He can bring a mesmerizing Omega and it's a tremendous gift to me. Breaking out of the cultural norms was an incredible liberation and gave us the ability to play in an entirely new way.

In truth, all of us are both Alpha and Omega. We are 100% made of consciousness (awareness) and 100% made of light (stardust), regardless of gender. However, almost all of us tend to have a primary orientation to one or the other, a home base we prefer to come back to, so to speak. Maybe we embody Alpha by day, running the show and kicking ass, but love to be enraptured by night as Omega. This will directly influence who we attract and who we repel and why sometimes things flow beautifully and other times you feel as though you are butting heads.

To fully understand polarity, we need to become familiar with both our Alpha and Omega qualities, and how they are affecting our relationship, both positively and negatively. We begin by understanding that between the two poles, there are 3 Ways of Relating.

13

The 3 Ways of Relating

There are three possible ways of relating to your partner in every moment: Alpha-Alpha, Omega-Omega and Alpha-Omega.

By understanding the three ways you can relate, you gain the ability to bring awareness and intentionality to the dynamic. You gain the ability to shape each moment as best serves your relationship, either into resonance (Alpha-Alpha/Omega-Omega) or polarity (Alpha-Omega) as you desire.

Being conscious of the three ways of relating allows you to stop judging your relationship or expecting it to look a certain way, and recognize the different dynamics that exist inside of relationships. While the two of you may not always be in polarity, you can just as easily embrace and enjoy resonance—and when resonance needs some spice or heat to break things up, you can dive into polarity to get that sexual spark going.

So let's look at how this works…

Alpha-Alpha: Powerful Partners

In Alpha-Alpha, both of you embody the purpose-driven, practical, work-mode qualities of Alpha. This puts you in resonance (not polarity).

> • The upside: this can lead to productive synergy as work partners. You use your combined talents to create amazing things in the world, whether that looks like managing a household, raising kids or running a business. In other words, you're both in charge and purpose takes precedence over intimacy.

> • The downside: this can lead to butting heads and power struggles because you will often find yourselves competing for the lead or holding your partner's nose to the grindstone with a laundry list of demands.

Alpha-Alpha is the domain of the modern power couple. It allows the two of you to team up and achieve things neither one of you could possibly achieve on your own. However, it can also unintentionally destroy erotic heat in the process. A great example of this could look like working side-by-side for months, then arriving on your dream vacation and being surprised to find out neither of you is in the mood for sex…at least not with each other.

Omega-Omega: Best Friends

In Omega-Omega, both of you embody the love-driven, emotional, pleasure-seeking qualities of Omega. This also puts you in resonance (not polarity).

> • The upside: this is the best-friend zone where you feel loved, supported and nurtured. You both prioritize relaxation and pleasure, such as cuddling on the couch, eating decadent food and tending to each other's emotional needs. In other words, no one's in charge and connection takes precedence

over purpose.

• The downside: this can lead to nobody being able to make a decision about anything, nothing getting done, balls dropping, business suffering and sharing pizzas instead of sex for pleasure.

Omega-Omega allows for lazing around with each other recovering when you are tired, stretched or pushed too hard by life. But while the loving communion of mutual Omega feels great for a while, it has a way of running its course.

This happens when it's time for someone to take charge...and no one does. If no one is holding the structure of the moment, it feels mushy, like things aren't going anywhere or you're both waiting for the other one to lead. You start to want more without really understanding why. You say things to your friends like, "He's very supportive. He has such a big heart. I don't know why I would be thinking about leaving him."

Omega-Omega is awesome for being friends and enjoying fun times together without any real responsibility or leadership. But if you also want to feel guided, seduced, and "taken" by your man, then you will need to learn how to inspire a shift in the dynamic when you crave something different (polarity).

Alpha-Omega: Passionate Lovers
In Alpha-Omega, one of you embodies Alpha—the witness who creates the structure of the moment. The other embodies Omega—the love-light that brings the energy to the moment. This puts you in polarity (not resonance).

In the same way that opposite magnets attract, Alpha-Omega gives us the foundation for passion to thrive and deep fuck to ensue. It gives you the ground for Alpha to provide the river banks while Omega brings the gushing flow.

- The upside: this creates intense passion. By your differences, you feel an almost insatiable attraction to the other person. The desire to merge with them sexually is so powerful, you could stare at the ceiling all night thinking of nothing but your next encounter.

- The downside: this can lead to an absence of resonance in both friendship and partnership. While the lovemaking is great through the intense sexual charge of opposites uniting, those opposite natures can lead to a complete lack of harmony outside of the bedroom. In other words, your partner, because he or she is so different from you, may seem perplexing, difficult to get along with or even intolerable...whenever you're outside a sexual moment.

Alpha-Omega enables you to feel sexually fulfilled beyond your wildest imagination, no matter how long you have been with your partner. But remember, polarity and resonance are not the same thing. Just because you have a strong sexual charge, do not assume you will feel that best-friend vibe or even a strong partnership. Alpha and Omega are opposites and while they attract, they have different needs and relate in different ways, which can lead to conflict.

For example, when you're in Omega, Alpha may feel emotionally unavailable, possibly even cold. When you're in Alpha, Omega may feel emotionally overwhelming, possibly even crazy.

While the differences can be maddening outside of intimacy, they are necessary within the sexual occasion. Alpha-Omega creates an overpowering effect. It is physics. When you embody these opposing forces, it will almost always lead to sparks. It can happen accidentally with a total stranger; it can happen intentionally with a lifetime lover.

Long-term relationships require us to find both polarity and resonance. If you're raising kids, both of you are working, or running a household together, your daily interactions will require moments of resonance for function to flow. Similarly, if you are unable to shift gears and set "work-mode" aside, you will find yourselves living without polarity. To have both resonance and polarity present in your relationship requires being intentional in how you relate.

We spoke earlier about how the modern woman is embodying Alpha qualities more often these days. The fluidity of gender roles has made polarity much harder to find than it was in the 1950s. But let's be clear: we're not saying you need to go back to the 1950s way of relating! The key to bringing polarity back has nothing to do with women giving up their power or men no longer softening their hearts, but building upon these newfound freedoms and offering something more. We do this through intentional relating, which empowers us to shift the dynamic as desired.

This is a wonderful empowerment for the awakened woman. Rather than lamenting there are "no good men," or seething with resentment when her husband behaves poorly, she takes responsibility for the way the men in her life are showing up around her. If they aren't cutting it, she knows there is a lot she can do to shift the dynamic, simply by shifting how she shows up.

To navigate these waters requires an ability to shift the relationship dynamic at will. This skill is what we call energetic agility.

14

Energetic Agility:
The Key to Having It All

The first thing to recognize about shifting the dynamic is that Alpha and Omega are not fixed states of being. You can shift from one to the other at will if you cultivate the skill we call energetic agility.

Energetic agility is the secret sauce to keeping intimacy alive inside of modernized gender roles. Agility means you are skilled in both Alpha and Omega, and can pivot between the two embodiments at will, choosing whichever best serves the moment. In other words, if things are feeling dull, you can bring back the heat anytime you want by noticing which embodiment would re-establish polarity and intentionally taking on that sexual pole.

When Justin and I first started doing this, it wasn't easy because we didn't have a map. We endured some pretty disappointing drops in passion and harmony as we worked out agility. For example, one time I was doing the driving for us (I was offering Alpha), but Justin pumped the gas (he took over Alpha) then walked into the store for a drink. When we pulled out of the station, we heard the gut-wrenching sound of the gas nozzle ripping out of my tank and looked at each other exasperated. Neither of us had bothered to pull the nozzle out!

Who was at fault? We both felt like the other one was, as each of us saw the other as the Alpha role in that moment. I wanted to kill Justin. Justin wanted to kill me. (And the gas station manager probably wanted to kill us both!) But honestly, you couldn't really blame either of us. In a fast-moving stream of switching polarities, it felt terribly confusing a lot of the time.

When we were clinging to predictable extremes, it was easy to create polarity. We both knew our "role" and there was never any confusion on how to create heat. When we broke the mold and had a full spectrum of possible notes to choose from, we made some pretty off-key songs at first. But we stuck with it for three full years, dedicated to cracking the code.

The key we found was something we now call polarizing the moment. Polarizing the moment has you focus on the moment, not fixed ideas of gender or polarity (i.e., he does Alpha and she does Omega). Rather, it asks: what does the moment require for the greatest love flow?

Rather than seeing polarity as something that is fixed, you see polarity as a dance which occurs moment to moment, each partner feeling into the situation and deciding which sexual pole to offer based on what would best serve the moment. In other words, in each interaction where we want polarity, we feel the other, know what they are offering and polarize it.

The way we gracefully make the shift is by using energetic agility. Again, we aren't fixed on a sexual pole, we are fluid, able to easily shift from one to the other as the moment requires. Sometimes, to achieve polarity, it's best to embody the opposite of what our partner is currently offering. Other times, you can create polarity by inspiring your partner to switch their sexual pole. In other words, if your partner is in Omega and you want them to move into Alpha, not you, you do this by embodying Omega way more than they are, thereby naturally polarizing them into Alpha.

For example, if Justin is in a state of productivity, focus and self-discipline (Alpha qualities), and I want to create polarity, I can easily do so by dropping into my natural tendency toward Omega. At the same time, if Justin has a moment where he loses his clarity of consciousness and becomes emotional, I don't criticize him for losing power or open a therapeutic examination of what is going on. I simply recognize he is in Omega, and that Omega isn't serving him in the moment…and then lovingly polarize him back to Alpha.

How I do this is by out-Omega'ing him. I literally go deeper into Omega than he is. This can look like letting my body flow more than his body is flowing, being less decisive than he is, feeling more feelings than he does, relinquishing direction completely (even if he's not offering it yet), and in every way occupying the Omega pole more than he is. At some point, my extreme Omega will literally polarize him into Alpha. By intentionally not taking control and not running the show, I will create such a big void that he has no choice but to step in and run the show. Boom, now he's back into Alpha.

The next thing he knows, he's feeling full of power again, and it didn't have to turn into a fight, or an over-analysis of our relationship dynamics. A yogic move of love that restored balance was all that was needed. And it returned the moment to love for both of us. This is energetic agility.

If I wanted him to go into Omega, how I would out-Alpha him is by making my spine straighter than his, becoming more grounded than he is and breathing deeper than he is. If I really wanted to polarize him, I would look him square in the eye and, in the most commanding, sexy way possible, tell him to "get over here."

I love the fact that I can go into Alpha, kick ass and be fully embraced in that pole. Like many women, I've spent so much time thinking I had to hide the "lady boss" parts of myself if I ever wanted to feel desired by men. In this relationship, I never have to hide those parts. In fact, Justin shows me how beautiful I am when I'm in full power, and it allows me to feel sexy in this place. Likewise, Justin gets to feel valued in Omega. He gets a break from having to always toe the Alpha line for us both, to always be in control and to make all the decisions. This is energetic agility, too.

What has been remarkable for us is the experience of true, unconditional love, which opened through this fluid switching of roles.

To train yourself to move between Alpha to Omega takes practice, no doubt. It takes awareness, knowing which pole you are occupying and what is needed with your partner. It takes patience, letting him play Alpha even if you feel you could do it better. And it takes practice to master the capacity to switch. You cannot expect a basketball player to learn a layup in the middle of the playoffs. You cannot expect yourself to find Omega in a Super Bowl moment. It takes practice to cultivate the muscle memory to execute a layup properly. It takes practice to cultivate the muscle memory of Omega's pleasure and juiciness to bring it with ease after a long day of Alpha work.

Just imagine daily life for the average woman. No matter what job you have, whether it is running a law office or running a household, you are highly valued for your mindfulness and ability to problem-solve. Whether you are managing employees or children, you serve best by not getting emotional, pulling yourself together and rising above the fray. You spend several hours a day sitting at a desk, in a car or at the computer—your body molded into stillness. If you look at the embodiment that best serves your life, it is Alpha. Every single thing you do with your day executes better if you bring Alpha.

Now imagine what happens if you come home in Alpha mode and reach out for intimacy. Either you will polarize your man into Omega or you will compete for Alpha. If you want to play Alpha in the bedroom, this can work…but after a long-ass day of being in Alpha every single minute, there's a good chance you may want to experience Omega in your love relationship, which means you literally must relinquish Alpha and allow your man to take the lead. This is the only way he can ravish you. Without energetic agility, this will be difficult if not impossible for you, as being in Alpha all day makes it all too easy to stay there at home. With energetic agility you can recognize the need to switch and make it happen without feeling wrong or less for doing it.

This leads to the most important question, the one probably running through your head right now: how exactly do I do this?

15

Embodying Alpha & Omega

To get started, the first step is to understand how polarity works, the second is to identify which of the 3 Ways of Relating you're in, and the third is to shift your dynamic as desired using energetic agility, creating either resonance or polarity, depending on which best serves the moment.

That said, we know it's not always as easy as it sounds, and we did just say how much practice it takes. So let's look at some more specific techniques you can use to polarize the moment and master energetic agility. One of the best ways to identify and shift dynamics is to understand how we embody Alpha and Omega. In other words, what you can do, not with your mind but with your body, to cause the shift. This is the yoga, and the yoga is where the real results take place. It is the difference between knowing what to do, and actually doing it.

Embodying Alpha

When you embody Alpha, you are the one taking the lead. You are the one directing the moment and deciding what needs to be done. You assume responsibility over others, and prioritize the purposefulness of getting things done: earning money, paying bills, providing for the family, etc. Any parent caring for a child, or any child caring for their parent, will find themselves in many moments of Alpha, being the one "holding the moment," responsible for the welfare of those they look after. In the sexual occasion, this could be thought of as the dominant or the "top."

The physical embodiment of Alpha is structure. Imagine the posture of someone who feels confident, strong, grounded, trustable, purposeful—straight spine, piercing gaze, full breath, rock-solid stance (you couldn't push them over). Historically, this was the domain of the masculine.

Embodying Omega

When you embody Omega, you sensitize to an extreme degree. You feel the impact of each moment, and vulnerably express your heart's authentic truth. You value relationship and love flow, making room for connection with family, friends and an intimate partner. Your desire is to nurture, and fill home and heart with abundance. You possess the capacity for heightened levels of intuition, deep compassion and full-bodied pleasure through ecstatic surrender. In the sexual occasion this could be thought of as the submissive or the "bottom."

The physical embodiment of Omega is flow. Imagine the posture of a person who is so surrendered into the felt sensation of the moment that they allow it to move them completely. This could look like music playing and they automatically begin to dance, or a sunset drawing tears of awe. The essential Omega posture is awakened permission to unleash the body in movement and emotions in expression. Hips, belly, arms, throat, eyes, lips, even the fingertips are alive with sensation and responsive. The entire body—physical to subtle—takes part in the dance of life. Historically, this was the domain of the feminine.

Remember, Alpha and Omega are not fixed states of being. You may naturally shift between Alpha and Omega several times throughout the day. You may also rest as a blend of the two sometimes, maybe 70% of you Alpha and 30% Omega. It is helpful to think of Alpha and Omega as a spectrum and continually observe where you land moment to moment, scenario to scenario.

Imagine a horizontal line that represents a spectrum, and splitting that line in half. The left side of the spectrum represents Omega, while the right side of the spectrum represents Alpha.

Omega   Alpha

The only thing that exists on the extreme ends of the spectrum is pure consciousness (Alpha) and pure light (Omega). All human beings land somewhere in between and, depending upon the moment, we may relate more with the consciousness aspects of self (Alpha), or we may relate more to the love-light aspects of self (Omega).

Another thing to consider is that all of us are multidimensional beings. You might have a mind that is incredibly oriented toward Alpha and a body that is highly oriented towards Omega. Your partner might have a mind that is oriented toward Omega and a body that is oriented toward Alpha. That would create perfect polarity in mind and body.

Alpha and Omega are also relative, heavily influenced by the people we surround ourselves with. Because it's all relative, the best way to find out where you stand on the spectrum in any given moment is by comparison. For example, stand next to your man, and you may feel like the more Omega person, but stand next to Marilyn Monroe, and you may feel like the more Alpha person.

Chances are likely that if you are in a polarized relationship, your partner will show up as the opposite of you in many areas. For this reason, you may find yourself occasionally attracted to members of the same sex even if you've never thought of yourself as a homosexual. In this case, the person you feel attraction toward is likely embodying the opposite sexual pole as you.

As a fun way to discover your primary home-base (Alpha or Omega), consider the following differences in how Alpha and Omega experience nourishment.*

Alpha Empties

Alpha is most nourished by emptying, such as spending time alone, resting as consciousness in still meditation, and enjoying competitive and/or relaxing experiences.

Omega Fills

Omega is most nourished by filling up, such as eating decadent food, spending lots of time with loved ones in conversations that have no end, and enjoying creative and/or mystical experiences.

Where do you fit? Think about your current or past partners - what kind of nourishment did they prefer?

Write down your answers.

*If you'd like to take a quiz to find out where you fall on
the spectrum, go to www.AwakenedWomansGuide.com/resources
and take that quiz now. At the end of the quiz, you will receive a
detailed report to interpret your results.

When we understand the difference between how Alpha and Omega relate to life, we gain the ability to understand ourselves better and to give our partner a lot of latitude in how they need to spend their time to feel the best. In other words, as Omega, we recognize Alpha's need for space, purpose and freedom. As Alpha, we recognize Omega's need for connection, romance and love.

Notice, if you found yourself in the Alpha-oriented pole, did any judgments come up about whether that makes you unlovable? These are important limiting beliefs to question.

A woman in Alpha can gift her man in many ways, whether that is offering him advice from the clarity of her perspective, inspiring him through life achievements of her own or even handling the driving because she is better at it. The sky's the limit for the fluid couple.

Conversely, a man in Omega can bring the flow of love into the relationship by setting up a gorgeous home environment to greet her after a long day of work, cooking nourishing meals, or even tending to her heart and body with sensitivity after she has pushed herself a little too hard in her Alpha ways. There's no judgment there either. All that matters is looking at where each other's talents lie and using them to benefit your life together.

Once you begin to understand the embodiments of Alpha and Omega, you can then use energetic agility to cultivate the ability to shift out of your comfort zones and habits to create something new. It may be awkward at first, but you get better with practice. Here is a real-life example.

Love Conflict #6: Ava's In Charge...and Undersexed

Ava found herself once again in a fight with her husband Troy. It seems like all they do these days is butt heads. Ava and Troy run a business and household together so they often clash over important decisions. When Troy gets exasperated with the fighting, he avoids the house and spends inordinate amounts of time with his friends. Ava can feel him keeping his distance and it pisses her off because it leaves her to handle all of the work around the house, kids and business.

To everyone else, their life appears to be great with a successful business and well-adjusted kids, but Ava and Troy are both at their wits' ends intimately. The only time they spend in the same room is at night before bed. But even then, they sit on the bed, laptops open, pounding away at email until one of them falls asleep and the other turns out the light and stares at the ceiling wondering if the relationship has run its course.

Love Solution # 6: Soften Into Omega

Notice the dynamic: Ava and Troy are stuck in Alpha-Alpha. It would make sense this happened. They spend most of their relationship working on their business and raising a family together, both of them in Alpha.

If Ava wants to bring the juiciness back and motivate Troy to step up and handle things (both in and out of the bedroom), she would need to move into the Omega-playing role. Troy had been letting Ava take the lead for so long because he hated the hassle of fighting her for it. Ava would need to implement some energetic agility for the situation to change.

By relinquishing the need to be in charge, she would create the space for Troy to step in and take over. By softening into receptivity, she would create the opening for Troy to ravish her. Troy may not do any of it perfectly at the start—he may not ever do it perfectly. Ava may have to bite her tongue, thinking she could do it better. But if Ava continually jumps in and tells Troy what to do, she'll chase Troy right out of the Alpha role.

Realizing this, Ava began to create space for Troy to show up. It wasn't easy at first. She had to let a few balls drop and deal with Troy doing things his own way. However, she began to see that Troy loves to be her hero. She began to notice him doing way more around the house beyond what she even asked him to do. By her having to handle less, she started to feel herself in the "mood" again and their nightly rendezvous in the bedroom became a whole lot more interesting for both of them.

Takeaway: If you hang back and let him find the lead, you change the picture entirely. By going into Omega, you not only create the space for him to step up; you actively show him how his lead feels. Even if it feels terrible, you expressively show that. He sees your pain and (ideally) course corrects. Over the course of the relationship, he learns to lead you better and better. Eventually, you get a man who can lead you better than you can lead yourself.

For polarity to sizzle, one partner must relinquish all of their Omega qualities, while the other relinquishes all of their Alpha qualities. In the mutual void that is created, guess who fills it? The opposite pole, i.e. your partner. When the two of you come together as the opposite poles, both will feel "completed" in the subtlest but most powerful of ways. This is ecstatic union. This is the sexual charge of polarity.

In order to switch from Alpha to Omega in the middle of the day, you can break your directional mindset and soften into your body—even if just for a few moments. Maybe you caress your thigh, give your man that "look" and he walks over, takes you into his arms, looks into your eyes and says, "You're beautiful." Then boom, you go right back into Alpha-Alpha, right back to work, and the two of you resume power-couple mode.

Justin and I take "love breaks" like this all the time. This is a central part of our daily practice. This is what makes running a business together fun. You can do this sort of practice two, 10 or 20 times a day and make it as creative as you like—you get to choose.

For women like Ava, it is a great gift to know that no matter how rough a relationship gets, the intentional embodiment of Alpha-Omega can bring back the heat.

Where most couples go wrong is:

1. They are unaware they've entered this dynamic with their partner.
2. They are looking for intimacy in moments of Alpha-Alpha, which is a place they will not find it.
3. They get stuck in Alpha-Alpha and have no idea how to transition into a different relationship dynamic, so both partners feel irritated by one another, stressed and dried up, and need to find release elsewhere (i.e., in alcohol, porn, food, TV or other people).

Here's the way out of those scenarios:

1. Become aware that you are in Alpha-Alpha.
2. Recognize that polarity does not thrive here, and either accept that or shift gears.
3. If you choose to shift gears, cultivate the energetic agility to do so by knowing the embodiments of Alpha and Omega and animating the sexual pole which brings back polarity.

Energetic agility is beyond a simple skill. It is a cultivation in that it takes more than just skill; it also requires awareness, willingness, spiritual maturity, discipline and practice. Once you gain the basic competency, it actually becomes fun. And you get the reward of super hot, delicious sex energy whenever you want to create it. For me, being able to work with Justin, pal around with him and experience him as the hottest lover I've ever had is my definition of having it all. It makes the work on cultivating agility worth every bit of effort.

Through His Eyes: The Beauty of Vulnerability, by Justin

Alpha-Alpha is the dynamic for taking care of business. It isn't the appropriate time for intimacy, or melding hearts or being lazy. When Londin and I are in Alpha-Alpha, you can feel the juiciness of love's flow dry up pretty quickly as the two of us gear up for action. We'll work side-by-side for 16 hours straight some days. We absolutely love it, despite the momentary sacrifice of sexual attraction that occurs.

But there will be times for Londin and me when Alpha-Alpha gets so intense, one of us has a breakdown. Emotions run so high that one of us needs to disengage completely or loses it. Too much Alpha-Alpha on any person makes them hard, and void of pleasure and life force. Man or woman, it's critical our bodies are nourished with Omega's love flow from time to time. This is where energetic agility can save the day, and the relationship.

For example, while working on this book together, Londin hit an edge. After months of working tirelessly and feeling the pressure of both of us wanting this book to be the best it could be, she cracked one afternoon while we were writing together. When Londin is in Alpha, she is sharp as a tack. She thinks clearly and feels level-headed. When she starts to crack, she becomes overwhelmed, stops thinking clearly and starts getting emotional.

After years together, I can usually sense these moments coming. When I feel one approaching, I know if I match her mood or become defensive, the moment will turn into a bloodbath. Instead, in the most loving way I can, I let her know that she has hit an edge and needs to unplug. Sometimes, she fights me initially, but if I lovingly hold my ground, she is able to find the permission to surrender her Alpha role, and let me take the lead. In this moment, the book momentarily forgotten, she pops out of Alpha and into Omega. Landing in Omega, she can feel herself again. The emotions come flooding back and she turns into a puddle of tears, helpless, soft and open. These have become some of my favorite moments in the relationship. There is little as delightful as a woman who is so passionately in touch with her heart, and allows you to see it fully, without any attempt to hide it.

In this moment, Londin steps outside to be with her tears, and I can tell this is the perfect opportunity for us to re-establish intimacy. So after a few minutes, I put down my work and calmly follow her outside.

She cries an ocean. I lovingly encourage her emotions with the quality of my presence. I welcome them with an open heart, not needing her to toughen up, or stop crying, or for the moment to change at all. I just hold her with my gaze as she sits there, pouring out her heart. All I can see is how deeply she cares, and how vulnerable she has become.

This nourishes me like nothing else. I let her tears run through me, as if they are washing my soul like rain. I delight in holding Alpha-Omega in this moment—a very needed, rejuvenating experience for both of us. Here, intimacy returns.

Sometimes, the attraction runs so deep in these moments that work goes on pause, and we transition into lovemaking from there. Book? What book?

16

Everlasting Love Doesn't "Just Happen"

Romance movies like to suggest that when you meet the perfect partner, you end up "lucky in love." As much as we might all wish it worked that way, in reality, attracting and sustaining this level of relationship, involving both deep resonance and thrilling polarity, takes a lot more than luck.

There are two key things to know about the mechanics behind everlasting love:

> 1. Manifesting this level of loving actually begins with the self, in what we call "Solo Practice."
> 2. It's always going to feel like your partner isn't practicing, or at least not at the level you wish they would.

Let's look at each of these now.

Solo Practice

As we've seen, energetic agility is the secret sauce to keeping things hot when there are multiple dynamics at play, particularly in long-term relationships. To be masterful at agility, you must possess fluidity in both Alpha and Omega. It takes dedicated practice to achieve that kind of agility. As we mentioned earlier, you can't expect yourself to find Omega in a Super Bowl moment if you can't remember the last time you embodied Omega.

When your essence wants to play Omega and your habits, patterns and closures keep you in Alpha (or vice versa), that is when you suffer. If you can't find one pole or the other by yourself, you certainly won't be able to find it with your partner present. Therefore, the place to develop your yogic embodiments of Alpha and Omega is in consistent solo practice.

If you are not taking time to practice, you may get stuck in one mode or the other. You may be stuck in Alpha and you cannot give up the lead no matter how hard you try—thus feeling tight, numb and not in the mood for love. From here, trying to find Omega in a moment of intimacy can feel like trying to push a stalled car up a hill. Or you could be stuck in Omega where you cannot motivate if you try—unable to exercise, rein in overeating or do what is necessary to move forward in your career.

What is beautiful is to feel agile and "light on your feet" like an athlete, capable of bringing whichever embodiment best serves the greater good. The embodiments will be available for you when you want them most—namely, the Super Bowl moments.

How much solo practice is needed at any given time will depend on the circumstances of your life and how consistent you are with your practice from day to day. For example, if a stressful week of intense computer work has locked your body into frozen stiffness and you notice there is nothing sexy going on with your man, you know it's time for solo practice. How much will depend on how long it takes to feel juicy again. If you've been practicing regularly and the muscle memory of Omega is readily at hand, it may only take one great song to unstick the tensions and get you back into pleasure. If your practice has been lacking, it may take five hours of dedicated Omega work to feel juicy again. The more you practice, the easier it is. The more you slack, the more time it takes to recover agility.

So, let's look at an example of a beginner solo practice for each embodiment.

Omega Beginner Solo Practice

A solid Omega solo practice means you never allow yourself to get too tight, rigid, or numb so it would take an entire weekend retreat to unwind. There needs to be a certain minimum of self-care woven into your life, such that you are never that far away from feeling good in your body.

Here's a simple practice you can begin doing right away:

1. Find a quiet place where you will be undisturbed, and set out a yoga mat or blanket.

2. Create a playlist of songs you love that is at least 15 minutes long.

3. Take a few deep breaths as a way of dropping out of your mind and into your body.

4. Stand or sit on the mat and begin moving your body to the music in a slow pleasurable way. That could be stretching your hamstrings, spreading your toes or twisting left and right. The only requirement is to keep moving and not freeze or start making to-do lists in your mind. Keep your attention on your body. Keep it based in pleasure. Try moving in ways you've never moved before in order to break the habitual patterns which lock your body tight. If you already have a yoga or movement practice, avoid doing those moves. You are looking to be spontaneous here and explore new territory in your expression. Move for the entire 15 minutes.

5. Stay committed. Even if you feel bored, numb or distracted, do not get off the mat no matter what. It may not feel enjoy-

able and this is normal. Sometimes when we have a great deal of residual tensions in our body, practice feels like work. It takes discipline and it pays off. If you stay in the practice long enough, the tensions will unwind, and the body will release.

The key is to set aside time to reclaim pleasure in the body and re-open the pathways of love. The more often you do this by yourself, the easier it will be to find Omega when you're with your partner.

Alpha Beginner Solo Practice

You know a solid Alpha solo practice is needed if you are such a plea-sure bunny that it becomes hard to find any self-discipline to get work done, care for your body, control your caloric intake, and so on. Alpha is an incredible resource to help you "get it together."

Here's a simple practice to begin doing right away:

1. Get those gym shoes out. Alpha embodies the qualities of structure, discipline and direction, so when you want to get back into Alpha, it's time to work out.

2. Go work out. You can take a walk if working out is new to you or head to the gym and lift weights if you are more experienced. Lower body moves like squatting and deadlifts are particularly grounding and helpful for switching gears energetically. Even if it feels incredibly difficult and sober-ing, keep moving until you feel your nervous system switch gears. You will know this happened when you suddenly drop into the moment and find it easier to exert energy.

3. Head home and get all the shit done that was piling up, such as returning emails, setting up schedules or whatever other Alpha-mode tasks you have been ignoring.

You will likely find it's much easier to do these tasks after a sweaty, hard workout.

When my solo practice is up to par, I am as skillful at Omega as I am at Alpha. When both Alpha and Omega are well nourished and at my fingertips, I have the chance at agility, with the ease of switching from one to the other at a moment's notice.

Can you see how it works? You develop wholeness in solo practice—your own Alpha creating river banks for your own Omega flow. Then, in partner practice, you relinquish one of the poles to come together with your partner in polarity—one of you is the river bank, the other the flow of the river.

As you navigate this dance, another benefit of solo practice is that it constantly invites your essence forward. It allows you to know and operate from your deepest truth. This is key to attracting a well-matched intimate partner.

With a strong solo practice, you are not coming to love from need or desperation. You are not deficient in Alpha and therefore demanding Alpha from your partner. Quite the contrary, you are whole unto yourself, and you voluntarily relinquish Alpha to allow him to fill that role. Coming from these cultivations, the loving you offer your partner has a majesty to it. It elevates beyond the subtle hostilities, power games and tit-for-tat bickering which is inherent in dependency dynamics.

For this to work, you must be serving something larger than your own agenda. If you never allow your man to go into Omega because you are afraid he will get stuck there, you will not be able to polarize the moment. It doesn't matter who plays which role—the woman could play Alpha and the man could play Omega, or vice versa. In all cases, when you create opposites in body, mind, and spirit, and then put them together, you get massive sparks.

This leads to the million-dollar question we get asked all the time:

"What if my partner isn't practicing?!"

17

What If My Partner Isn't Practicing?!

Guess what? It's always going to feel like your partner isn't practicing...even when they are!

Justin and I see this regularly in our workshops. A man and a woman may be experiencing a moment of heart connection more deeply than anything either of them has experienced before. Then, in the very next moment, the woman will say, "It was an amazing experience, but he did not do X, Y or Z." Even if the moment of connection is transcendent, for the love-driven being, it's not enough, and there is always more to be had.

The nature of Omega is that there is never enough love. While this may sound like neediness, it's not. Instead, it is an authentic yearning of the heart, which comes from a beautiful place. Omega has an intuitive knowing of boundless, infinite love—a love so divine that no experience on this earthly plane could ever match it.

If you're the love-driven partner in your relationship, no matter what kind of love you get, it's natural to want more. We call this eternal yearning.

Here's the catch: Alpha has an eternal yearning as well, but in a different way. The purpose-driven being craves unbound freedom to the same extent that the love-driven being craves unbound love. No matter how much money they make, accomplishments they achieve, or power they hold, it will never completely fulfill the desire to know absolute freedom.

This desire often shows up as wanting many different options. We particularly see this in Alpha's desire for variety in intimacy. The Omega-playing partner may be offering every nuance of radiance, doing backflips of love offerings, and the Alpha-playing partner will still wonder what they're missing. This can be maddening to the love-driven being, particularly in long-term monogamy.

Can you see the dilemma in relationship? One partner yearns for more connection, while the other fights for freedom. In other words, the desire for more doesn't necessarily mean your partner isn't practicing, and you will both likely experience wanting more, whether your partner is practicing or not.

This happens in our relationship at times. As the love-driven partner, I can spend the whole day with Justin, make love to him multiple times, and then, in the moment when he dials back into work, my heart is already aching for more. Rather than writing this off as crazy, I recognize it as my eternal yearning for love, and let myself feel the ache fully. I have compassion for it, and Justin does, too.

If Justin felt like my complaint was an attack against him, or a demand to love me more, he would be insanely frustrated by my eternal ache. Instead, we don't let it trigger either one of us. I don't make Justin feel wrong that I'm still wanting more love. And he doesn't make me feel wrong that I'm still wanting more love. We use it as a source of great humor and fun, wrestle each other to ground, crack into belly laughs at the absurdity of it all, and then go about our day.

Here's a real-life example of Omega suffering Alpha's insatiable desire for more:

Love Conflict #7: Amber's Nurse Outfit Backfires

Amber goes out and buys a wig and a sexy nurse outfit to delight her man, Drew, in a surprise evening of romantic role-play. Drew enjoys every last second of it. The next morning they roll out of bed, more in love than ever, and saunter over to the local breakfast joint.

When they sit down at their table, Amber notices Drew rubber-neck the short skirt the waitress is wearing. Suddenly furious, she thinks to herself, "Are you fucking serious? How could you do that after I go out of my way to meet your every sexual need?" As coffee arrives, Amber is not only fuming—she begins to internally collapse, wondering if she's not enough for Drew. This thought causes her to shrink on one hand, and enrage on the other. She silently vows that she is never doing anything for his sorry ass again, and spends the rest of the meal seething with resentment and withdrawing completely.

Love Solution #7: Embrace Eternal Yearning

This is a classic case of Alpha's eternal yearning for freedom butting heads with Omega's endless desire for more love. Without an understanding of the opposing forces of freedom versus love, Amber has no choice but to decide she's "not enough" and to harbor resentment.

Amber needs to avoid falling into the trap of making Drew's sexual yearning about her inadequacy. Believing there is anything she can do to quell his appetite for radiance is a myth and will have her bending over backwards to no avail. It is like trying to fill a tank that has a hole in the bottom. It won't work.

Instead, she can recognize that it's Drew's inability to give her unwavering presence that hurts, not her inadequacy of deserving it. No matter how much her heart hurts, she must resist going inward and instead express her emotion fully, showing Drew how much it hurts for him to lose presence. In this way, she stays open in the moment, confident in herself, and also serves Drew by awakening him to the moment.

You may wonder how on earth anyone can make a relationship work. With dueling eternal yearnings at play, it will always feel like your partner isn't measuring up. The key is to have compassion for these parts of our partners and ourselves. When we stop trying to fix this as if it's a problem to be solved, and instead do the yoga, we gain access to a level of liberation that is life-changing.

The yogic approach is to recognize and embrace that it's never going to feel like enough, for Alpha or Omega. It is to recognize that it's not about projecting that piece onto your partner, but instead using it as the fuel to drive your love.

Rather than trying to solve your endless hunger for more, you can learn to accept this aspect of yourself. Allow your eternal yearning (and your partner's) to deepen you, enliven you and drive you toward the richest life experience.

And remember: people are human. We are all going to be oblivious, self-centered, half-assed and distracted from time to time. This is not about perfection. Perfection brings a stiffness and rigidity that falls on its own sword. It's practice hijacked by ego. Rather, hold these practices with ease and compassion, and be mindful if you are getting tyrannical. A dose of love and humor goes a long way here.

Even though it may not feel like it, the way your partner shows up is usually a reflection of how you are showing up. In whatever way you feel their closure, you are usually matching them in an equal yet opposite closure of your own. For example, if you are dating and you attract nothing but wishy-washy men, you might want to look at whether you are hiding your authentic heart's truth—a reciprocal yet slightly different way of avoiding love.

By looking at this principle of reciprocity, we can learn something from every partner, every date. We stop blaming our partners for unpleasant patterns in relationship. We recover our power to influence the quality of our intimacy and we inch closer and closer to a sacred relationship as we unwind our own blocks to it.

Along the same line, it's important to be honest with yourself. Instead of automatically assuming there is a problem if sparks are not present, be willing to own the moments when you don't actually want to do the work it takes to create sparks. As you saw in the Love Conflict, it does require work. You may or may not want to do the work all the time. Plus, how much polarity you require for your relationship to feel fulfilling will be different for every couple. Some couples want polarity all the time. Some couples require very little polarity to be happy in their relationship. Most of us shift in between, depending upon everything else we have going on at the time.

If you are the love-driven being, you cannot expect the purpose-driven being to sweat the relationship as much as you. Do not hold it against him if he doesn't want to read this book, for example. And do not hold it against him if he's not as excited to implement the practices as you are. Just because he's not obsessing on your relationship, or approaching it exactly the way you are, it doesn't mean he's not practicing. And it doesn't necessarily mean there's a problem.

A man who can and will receive your fullness will be interested in developing consciousness, choosing love, and having integrity in the world—and you can bet he'll do it in his own way. His work on himself may not look like yours, but it will be consistent, trustworthy and devoted to growth.

Also, it's important to realize that sacred relating can appear like "leap frogging" at times. You will be ahead for a while and waiting for him to catch up. Then he will be ahead for a while and waiting for you to catch up. This happens regularly with Justin and me. While it's very frustrating to be the one in the lead, I thank my lucky stars for his patience when I'm the one trying to catch up. We are constantly inspiring each other forward and loving compassion goes a long way toward longevity.

When to Leave the Relationship

Sometimes it's not the case of differing orientations to practice. Sometimes it's the case that your partner really isn't practicing…not at all. Maybe you have a partner who doesn't want anything to do with the yoga, or with any other kind of developmental work. Maybe you need him to grow to match your growth…and he's just not interested. When you want to grow and he consistently does not, there may really be a problem.

In this case, you may have truly outgrown your partner. The relationship was probably a fit when you first met, but now it feels like it is no longer a fit—and his disinterest in working on himself or on your relationship in any way may have become a "deal breaker" for you. If this happens, you may need to ask yourself some hard questions about whether to continue the relationship or move on.

If you do decide to move forward, make sure to support yourself in solo practice—not only will that reassure you of feeling uninterrupted love, it will prepare you to make the next relationship (whenever it shows up) a sacred one.

*** *Breathe* ***

Through His Eyes: What a Deep Man Is Looking For, by Justin

When you are attracted to an Alpha male, it's important to remember he is a purpose-driven being. His mission likely matters to him more than his relationship. This doesn't mean he doesn't love or value you. It means that when push comes to shove, he prioritizes his work in the world over intimacy.

This is important for women to recognize if they are interested in building a relationship with a purpose-driven man. If his relationship feels like a distraction from his mission, he will either suffer or leave.

Some men are able to find this perfect balance where their relationship serves both their desire for companionship and their pursuit of purpose. But for many men, it does not always feel this way. For them, it can sometimes seem as if the relationship is the one thing standing in their way. If a man feels his relationship is distracting him from the pursuit of his purpose, he will feel sabotaged by his woman. If that happens, he will likely do one of two things: he will either emasculate himself in an effort to make the relationship feel workable and forego his mission in life, or he will distance himself from his woman and possibly leave the relationship altogether.

A deep man is looking for a woman who can meet his depth, but rather than matching him in the depth of his presence, he wants her to meet him reciprocally, through her expression of radiance. His attention is drawn to a woman who radiates love-light from surface to deep. Most men will be drawn in by surface radiance, but a deep man will require radiance of being, and a woman that will inspire him to grow.

Through this growth, his purpose itself continues to deepen and evolve, and the integrity in which a man lives a life authentic to his heart's truth is reflected in his lover's eyes. It is she who shows him when he is on course and when he is not. To watch those eyes fill with light when he is succeeding in his mission is reason enough to devote himself to her for good.

18

Polarity Ain't Special
(And That's a Good Thing!)

Most importantly, do not immediately give up on your relationship if you have lost polarity.

It's easy to feel frustrated if you are not enjoying the sexual sparks you desire in your life. It's depressing to watch a relationship go from super charged to super dull. It can be confusing when you can go to a social gathering, have a conversation with a total stranger and feel more polarity with the stranger than with your partner. Don't worry. All of this is completely normal—and largely meaningless. We encourage you not to fall into the trap of making it mean something about your relationship.

It is not uncommon for couples to lose polarity here and there. Remember, familiarity breeds sameness and sameness puts you in the same sexual pole (resonance). This is why polarity is often strong in the beginning and fades over time. This is why you can feel huge polarity with a total stranger in passing and barely any for your husband of 20 years.

The best news is, a loss of polarity doesn't necessarily say anything about whether your relationship is good or bad. The whole point of Pillar II is to show you how easy it is to get polarity back, no matter how many years you have been having (or not having) sex with each other. Polarity between couples can be restored much faster than most realize.

Polarity is addictive, no doubt. Feeling that tingle in your belly for another is one of the best things about romance. However, people who think sexual attraction is something special become slaves to it. If you start to chase polarity, you will soon find yourself in the dynamic of dysfunction we call "relationship cycling" where you go from one fling or short-term relationship to the next, losing interest as soon as the sexual spark fades.

If you think polarity with another person means you are destined to be with them, you are screwed. There will always be another person across the party who could be "the one." Likewise, if you insist on polarity being present at all times with your partner, you will find yourself resenting them and feeling as if they are not practicing.

When polarity is missing, it's not helpful to play the victim, go searching for another or blame your partner or the relationship. What is helpful is to look at your own practice, to identify which sexual pole you are embodying, and to notice whether you are resonating your partner or polarizing them.

It is also helpful to remember that while polarity can be huge, it's not everything. I believe that the working knowledge and skill with polarity has been the reason Justin and I have stayed so hot for each other for so many years. But we can maintain polarity without it backfiring because we remember polarity is only one of the three pillars. Polarity is an important part of our partnership, but it isn't the only part. Our practice of polarity is grounded by presence, which we've already written about, and supported by devotion, which we'll get to shortly. Without any one of those three pillars and practices, we'd be struggling a lot more—with only one of them, we'd have broken up years ago.

When you realize that polarity says nothing about true love, you are free. You are free to create it whenever you want it with your chosen partner. And you are free to not make it mean anything when you feel it with someone who isn't your chosen partner.

Learning polarity can set you free from wondering whether you are still with the right person when polarity runs out, feeling afraid that one day you might feel trapped and unloved in your relationship, and fearing your current relationship might end up in the gutter of neutrality.

When you understand that magnetic attraction is a function of certain behaviors, you discover you always have the ability to create polarity at will.

19

The 9 Common Polarity Killers

Energetic agility is the art of creating polarity at will. But sometimes the best way to create polarity is simply to avoid killing it. In many situations with our partners, there are things we do, usually unconsciously, which absolutely destroy sexual charge and attraction. We call these polarity killers, and this chapter will teach you how to identify and avoid or defeat nine of the most common ones.

1. Complaining with a Closed Heart

By far the biggest polarity killer of them all is complaining with a closed heart. Nagging, shaming and nit-picking are all forms of this. They represent a situation where your partner can't win. You've already given up on him and now you're just pouring salt in his wounds. For him, it shows up as being scolded or shamed, often for something he didn't intend to do or didn't even know he was doing. And because your tidal wave of complaints offers him no opportunity to redeem himself, he's totally unmotivated to try. The solution to this problem is to show him how he's making you feel through presence rather than telling him by nagging or lecturing. By seeing the pain he's inflicting, he will suddenly be motivated to become a better man.

2. Talking Too Much

Another big polarity killer is unconscious conversation. As we already saw, chit-chat, gossip and mundane conversation put all the energy in the head and reduce awareness to the lower body. Whether it comes from Alpha or Omega, that's just not sexy. Remember, if energy is up in the head, it's not down in the genitals. That's going to be a buzzkill no matter who you are. If this is an issue for you, revisit the embodiment practices in previous sections.

3. Avoiding Eye Contact

If you can't handle a person's gaze, how on earth are you going to seduce them? Lack of eye contact is a serious polarity killer because it's a sign that you cannot meet the moment. In Alpha, you display an inability to penetrate the moment. In Omega, you display an inability to receive the moment. If you want powerful intimacy, Alpha needs to meet the moment fearlessly as consciousness. Omega needs to meet the moment fearlessly as love. Strong eye contact is a sign of fearless loving.

4. Getting Stuck in Roles

Another polarity killer is what we call getting stuck in roles, or bringing the same energy to your partner over and over. For example, if I'm a mother and I am constantly in mommy mode, I might forget that I still have access to seductress, queen or dominatrix. If I am a provider and I constantly toe the work line, coming home tired, I forget I have access to bad boy, secret agent and warrior. Just as you wouldn't want to eat the same thing for breakfast, lunch and dinner every day of the week, many of us don't want to feel the same energy from our partner all the time, every time. It can become quite the buzzkill. Don't be shy to explore different energies with your partner. You may be surprised how much they love it.

5. Hair Twirling and Nose Picking

Many of us have ways of relating to others that are unconscious and clumsy. This causes the other person pain, as we are not sensitive to the impact we are having when we go unconscious. Hair twirling, nose picking and other nervous habits represent a lack of body awareness, an indication that you have gone unconscious, even with yourself. It's okay to be nervous. It's not okay to let your nervousness sabotage a moment of connection. Intimacy occurs body to body. If you don't know how to be mindful with yourself, how could you be mindful with another? If you can't be bothered to take care of your own body, how could you intimately serve another person's body? The yoga teaches us to be awake in body, mind and spirit. Great lovers are artists of their bodies and deliberate with each and every gesture they make and breath they take. Try it and see how tremendously seductive it is.

6. Suppressing Power & Radiance

Another common polarity killer is suppressing power (if you are in Alpha) or radiance (if you are in Omega). In Alpha, to deny power is to suppress the embodiment of strength. You will lose potency sexually, and reduce your ability to succeed in the world. You pride yourself on being safe and agreeable, but do so by keeping yourself disempowered, you cannot earn the trust or respect of the people around you. To suppress radiance in Omega is to take care of everyone else's needs but your own. You may have a squeaky-clean house, but you haven't exercised in a century. If you don't care about sexual charge, none of this is a problem...if you want to experience the thrill of intense polarity, you need to more intentionally embody Alpha or Omega. If you continue to hide who you really are, you will attract others who are hiding as well.

7. Giving Alpha Direction

Sometimes we kill polarity by confusing the sexual pole we are occupying. For example, if we are the Omega-playing partner and we give Alpha direction, it's a major polarity killer. Leading is the domain of Alpha. To give direction is to get over there and do the job for him. You will both end up in Alpha. To restore polarity, let him take the lead as we described in the chapter on energetic agility. You might have to bite your tongue at the wayward direction he takes to get to the restaurant, but you enjoy the reward of a sexually charged date night once you get there.

8. Suppressing His Sex Drive

A big mistake many women make is to try to control the parts of their man that feel threatening to monogamy. For example, she might shame him for being horny, punish him for loving sex or tell him he's too much and needs to "tone it down." Suppress his sex drive and you both lose. He will have one of two choices: either emasculate himself and lose potency, or take his sexual energy further away from you and into secretive behaviors—porn, strip clubs with the guys and/or cheating. If you can enjoy his sexuality and not make him feel wrong for it, he'll be way more willing to direct it toward you.

9. Trying to Impress Alpha with Alpha

It's tempting to match strong Alpha presence with mindfulness. It seems logical to impress a smart man with your intellect or a successful man with your success. But remember, polarity comes from opposites. Rather than matching Alpha in mindfulness, intellect or power, what if you brought the gush of your juiciest Omega flow? What if you displayed your intense yearning for love? Contrary to popular belief, this won't drive him away, it will likely drive him crazy…for you.

As we spoke about at the beginning, we are not taught how to love. Much of what we learn about relationships are concepts that keep us in our heads or strategies that project us out of the right-now moment and into the past or future. The Yoga of Intimacy™ teaches us what we can do with our body, mind and spirit to create deeper, authentic connection. We learn how to be intentional in the way we show up to bring more love, sparks and desire.

Unless you're looking for them, chances are slim you would even notice you were doing any of these polarity killers. Rather, it would just feel as if one moment you were into each other, and the next moment you weren't. And without the skill to recover the moment, it would lead to an awkward end of the evening or a slow death of the relationship. The good news is, with awareness, you can recognize when you're killing polarity and course correct before you inadvertently suck the juice right out of your encounter.

20

Being Opened into the Divine
Through Lovemaking

Whether it's purposefully turning polarity on or accidentally turning polarity off, what it all comes down to is a choice in every moment of how you run your energy—Alpha or Omega—and noticing the impact it has. We have shown you several examples of what it looks like to practice energetic agility in day-to-day life or on a date with your partner. Now we want to show you what it's like to practice energetic agility in the bedroom. Namely, how do you actually receive the hot sex you might say you want? You surrender when you may not want to surrender. Here's a real-life story which happened recently with me and J...

This morning in lovemaking, I saw the face of God.

It takes a complete surrender for this to happen. There cannot be any tension in my body whatsoever. When I merge with the eternal through that level of surrender, I break into tears. The tears come from the uncensored flow of energy. They come from the deepest places in practice where a merger occurs with the divine, a visceral experience of love. In these moments, my pain dissolves, my heart opens and I burst into tears at the beauty of eternal love. Some people experience this realization during meditation or through drugs. Those who practice the yoga experience this through lovemaking.

It doesn't happen every time. Ironically, I wasn't even in the mood to have sex when it happened. It was our second session that day. I was already feeling satisfied when Justin approached me to make love again. I didn't really want to. But I did it anyway, my first expression of surrender.

Several parts of me try to resist: the part in me that doesn't want to have sex the second time, the part that thinks it's about orgasm and I already checked that box, the part that thinks it's all about me and I felt finished, and the part in me that performs, asking how I could possibly muster a show for Justin if I wasn't in the mood. But I relax all of that and I show up, the basic principle of the Yoga of Intimacy™… relax all of that and show up. You could apply this to almost anything as it relates to sacred relationship.

He takes off my pants and lays me down on the bed, showing me his erect cock. I had just been in the middle of ordering makeup off Amazon.com, two-day delivery, my favorite indulgence. Erect cock, new face primer, erect cock, new face primer—my mind batting back and forth. When I was single and given the opportunity to meet the erect cock of a man I adore, it was massively huge. But in a relationship for years and years and having already made really great love earlier in the morning, I look at that erect cock and I can feel the decision point…am I going to stay obsessed with my Amazon order, which was nearly finished and what if it quits out and, and, loose end! Or, am I going to turn my attention to the right-now moment with this hunk of a man ready to take me?

Can I literally turn off the gear which was turning over there at Amazon? In Alpha, I could not. I would need to complete my task before turning my attention to Justin. I could feel the Alpha part of me fighting to run the show right then and ask for some time before we made love. In Omega, a moment of connection with my man is far more important than anything else in the world and I can flow from one thing to the next. I decide to embody Omega. After all, I'm staring at the love of my life.

I put my hands around his cock and drop so deeply into the right-now moment that I can feel the skin-to-skin contact of my hand to his shaft. I use my "yes" to break my Alpha austerity, and find the pleasure that is Omega.

I ask myself, "What in this moment is feeling pleasurable to me?" I look for my yes. I must move my body to find it. I need to shake off the staring at my computer frozen in stillness. So I very subtly begin to allow my body to flow. I feel more turned on, but it's still mild.

Justin can feel that I'm not totally into it yet. He asks me what I need. I tell him I want to feel his pleasure to help me find my own. He tells me he needs me to suck in his cock all the way through my toes and fingers. As I begin to do this, I feel stuck in my thoughts and barely connected to pleasure at first, but Justin is loving what I'm doing, and it drops me into my body. I let the currents of energy begin to travel across my limbs, spreading into the bottoms of my feet, charging my arms and fingertips, my online shopping cart a distant memory. My body stretches open wide and the pleasure begins to surge.

I keep my body soft and my breath full, driving Justin crazy. This builds pleasure in his balls, helping him drop the sensation deep and wide into his body. I run even more energy across his body, spreading the currents through all of his limbs, helping him widen into the sensation, his whole body lit up by the electricity of pleasure.

At one point, all this opening and widening and deepening on both of our parts causes my vagina to become incredibly relaxed. The deepest inner parts of my pussy become soft and receptive. There is no bracing against his thrust whatsoever. I am literally mushy, wet and relaxed deep into my cervix.

Rather than focusing on the lips of my vagina tracking his shaft, I allow myself to feel my cervix touch and release the tip of his cock. His very specific rhythm, which is tuned to my every nuance, creates the space for me to build my pleasure. Each thrust creates a ripple that spreads across my entire body. I began to shift slightly left when I want the tip on the right and slightly right when I want the tip on the left and we move perfectly in sync as if he is feeling my body and I am feeling his. And then suddenly out of a demand for deeper penetration, my entire cervix wall opens wide and begins to suck his cock as far inside as it can.

The thrusting turns to stillness as my deepest aspect suction-cups him inside of me and just when it completes the suction, I explode and melt simultaneously into the most sacred surrender, into pure delicious unspeakable pleasure. Waves and waves roll through me with no real beginning and no real end, and the vibration of God overtakes my entire body as I continue to fill.

It is so tempting to clench during these moments, to close inward, to round forward, to squeeze the face. Any of that would clamp it down, shut it down and bring it back to the regular plane. But I've learned how to stay open, soft and completely surrendered in these moments. I've given up the fear of being annihilated in the surrender. And as a result, my body blows open into a force that pierces the veil, a force that is so healing it brings tears, a force that is so connected it resolves everything in the space. This force is love.

I let myself cry and sob and stay open and continue sucking on his cock with my pussy and he goes into waves of internal orgasm. And then to stillness. And we hang out for a moment, he inside of me and me annihilated, and we rest in that moment, gazing at each other's eyes.

Then he slowly pulls out and leaves me in pieces on the bed to slip off into some mixture between this world and another, my body completely limp, my mind completely off and my heart wide open.

I stay that way for hours, even through the afternoon. I can barely speak. Nothing seems to matter enough to speak. I am in awe of love and floating in the mystery.

Summary of Pillar II: Polarity

Without polarity, passion can fizzle quickly in a relationship. To have attraction and desire stay alive over time, you must learn how to generate polarity intentionally. It's as simple as embodying opposite sexual poles.

We all play Alpha and we all play Omega sometimes. It's our lack of clarity around which dynamic we are in that causes the biggest rifts in relationships. With this awareness, we empower ourselves to become co-creators of the moment, rather than victims of it. With energetic agility, we work in cooperation with our partner, co-creating magic by responding and playing with each other in a continually unfolding matrix of polarities and resonance.

This skill gives us the artistry to shift a moment from mundane to ecstatic, from tense to humorous, from dispassionate to loving. It puts the power back in our hands to have love feel delicious whether we are together for 30 days, 30 months or 30 years.

These principles allow you and your partner to see and honor one another as full-spectrum beings. The art is lovingly growing in both spectrums with one another indefinitely.

Inspire your partner into depth by how you show up to the moment. Use inspiration to draw your partner into you rather than shutting down or pulling away when they feel unable to meet you.

Never stop teasing each other, tantalizing each other and doing all the things you did naturally when you first met. Busy lives have a way of conspiring to deaden you to your body and the flow of passion in your relationship. Don't let it. Prioritize intimacy. Cultivate skillfulness and dedicate yourself to doing one thing each and every day to turn on your partner. Don't be afraid to work at it; remember, you've got your daily solo practice as your foundation. The dimensions of growth never end, even in old age. Love is always present, constant and evolving in its expressions.

To know how to inspire my man into Alpha and feel his lead superior to mine is a gift beyond measure. To have him there to help me sink into the pleasurable waters of Omega after an intense day of Alpha work, rather than turning to ice cream or wine, is a luxury which fills me up better than any sweet treat ever could. To be cherished in my Alpha energies, knowing my man finds me super hot when I'm kicking ass in the world and doesn't feel diminished in his power, is a treasure I waited my entire life for. And to witness my both my Alpha and my Omega serve my man, my community and the world is a life beyond my wildest dreams. I feel I get to have it all—a rocking career and a profound intimacy. And you can have this as well, through the practice of polarity.

When you offer the full force of your love-consciousness as a gift to your partner, your practice will inspire them to reciprocate with a kind of loving that is organic and natural. In the best moments of practice, neither one of you is thinking about what you are doing; you are just allowing your authentic hearts to move through you, to be received fully by the other. A being who loves you will respond with love, as love. It is our very nature. Give your love always and let your partner be inspired to step in to meet you, soul to soul.

Pillar II Practice: Part A.
Turned On in 90 Seconds

To have ferocious lovemaking be a regular part of your life, it requires both you and your partner to know exactly what to do to tease, excite and drive one another to the edge of sexual ecstasy.

All it takes is for Justin to whisper a few words into my ear, and I turn on like a light switch. My impulse to open my entire body to him becomes irresistible. It's these moments that I live for, ignited by one small, subtle invitation.

In order for the small invitations to have great impact, you must know what gets your partner going beyond the casual encounter. You may think you already know, but when you are together with the same person for years, what turns you on shifts and changes over time. Justin and I constantly put on a beginner's mind and ask the tough questions of each other. We call them the tough questions because it's not always fun to hear what your partner is needing, particularly if you take it personally. If you are going to ask your partner these questions, it's critical that you do not punish them for their honest answers. The idea here is to set down defensiveness and be open to new ideas. For example, if he tells you he needs you to move or dress in sexier ways, do not accuse him of not loving you as you are.

This practice has several steps and each step will be appropriate at different times for different people, depending on whether you are single, dating or in a long-term relationship. We invite you to read through the entire exercise to prepare your body and mind for when the moment is right for you to put it into practice. This exact sequence is available as a free guided audio where we take you and your partner through each direction so you don't have to stop and look at the page each step along the way. The link to the audio is below.*

Here is the practice:

1. What would turn you on in 90 seconds?

90 seconds may sound like too short a period of time to really turn someone on—but it can be done. And with practice, it can be done very well. The reason this practice is so effective is because you only have 90 seconds to imagine what it would take to go from walking through the front door after a long day of work to being in ecstatic union with your lover. There isn't a lot of wiggle room for fluff (i.e., "Hello dear, how was your day?"). This is about getting straight to the good stuff.

Take a moment now and feel into it. What would you need? Would you need your partner to greet you at the front door as you arrive home from work, penetrate your soul with a silent, piercing gaze, lovingly command you to "get over here," and lift you up off your feet, passionately pinning you up against the wall?

Maybe it's a certain kind of touch. Maybe it's something they say...or don't say. Maybe it's tender. Maybe it's fierce.

The question is: What would you need from your current or future partner to be turned on in 90 seconds?

Write down your answer.

_____

_____

_____

_____

_____

_____

2. What would your partner need to be turned on in 90 seconds?
For this next step, we invite you to find out what it would be for your partner. If you are currently single, we encourage you to practice by asking this question to a trusted friend (you might be surprised at how many amazing ideas they have of their own). If you are currently dating, we encourage you to only do this practice with someone you trust. And if you're in a relationship, we strongly encourage you to do this with your partner regularly.

Keep in mind, it really helps to give examples and ask lots of questions. Be as creative as you like to help them get their gears going. Here are some ideas (if you are asking a trusted friend, you can ask all the same questions just replace "me" with "your current/future partner."):

• What would you need from me to be turned on in 90 seconds?

• How would you like me to move my body? Would you need me to move slower or faster? Would you want me to be standing, sitting or laying down? Would you want me to crawl on all fours like a wild animal or move like a princess?

• What kind of clothing would you like me to wear? Would you prefer sexier outfits that show a lot of skin or more conservative clothes which make you want to know what lies underneath? Would you prefer I peel off my clothes as you watch or would you want to undress me yourself?

• How would you like to be touched? Would you like a soft touch or firm pressure on your body? Would you prefer no touching whatsoever?

• What would you want me to say to you? Would you want me to whisper quietly or command you?

Write down their answers.

3. Put It Into Practice

There is an art to bringing this practice to your relationship. Depending on the current state of your relationship, engaging in this kind of practice could feel thrilling and exciting, or it could feel challenging and bring up a lot of emotions. This practice can be suitable for all intimate partners, especially those couples who are struggling to bring passion back into the equation. It's just a matter of approaching things mindfully.

In order to do that, we must set a clear container.

Setting a Container

Setting a proper practice container is very important. It gives the practice a clear starting and ending point. Inside (and only inside) of this practice time, you and your partner are agreeing to participate fully. This means you are both committed to giving and receiving honest feedback and allowing full permission to make mistakes. If both you and your partner agree to these terms, then, and only then, should you move on to the next step.

For this particular practice you will more than likely want some privacy, so a restaurant may not be the best choice, but then again, we're not here to limit your creativity. You could plan to practice in the living room, the bedroom, the shower, or even the kitchen (if your 90-second fantasy includes utensils).

Once you've decided on a location, next you will need to set a specific amount of time. For this practice, we recommend you start with at least 20 minutes. This means each partner will get 10 minutes of practice. The best way to do this is to set an alarm at the halfway point so you and your partner know when to switch.

Setting a proper container also looks like eliminating all major distractions during your practice time. There is nothing, literally nothing, that sabotages a moment of intimacy like an unexpected phone call.

Televisions are off, phones are on silent, kids are asleep or out of the house, etc. If all this is agreeable to both you and your partner, then your container is set and you're ready to dive into practice.

Remember to be honest with yourself and your partner about your true desires. And don't be surprised if what you need is dramatically different from what your partner needs. This is common. These are great conversations to have as a couple. It is avoiding these types of conversations entirely that sometimes end up costing us the relationship. The act of simply giving yourself permission to say what you desire to each other is a huge step in opening the channels of real, raw and honest communication, which is the basis of sacred relating.

Pillar II Practice: Part B.
Turn On Your Partner in 90 Seconds

For this practice, you will learn how to turn on your partner in 90 seconds first, and then your partner will learn how to turn you on second.

There are three parts to this practice:

Part I. Learn how to turn on your partner in 90 seconds.

Part II. Turn your partner on in 90 seconds.

Part III. Receive your partner's feedback.

Then you will switch partners and repeat.

Part I. Learn how to turn on your partner in 90 seconds

Set the timer for 10 minutes. To begin, your partner will spend just a few short moments describing what they would need you to do in order to turn them on in 90 seconds. The way they need to do this is by saying, "I would need you to..." at the beginning of every instruction. It's very important that every piece of feedback is delivered this way. A few examples are:

- I would need you to stand like this...

- I would need you to look at me like this...

- I would need you to say this...

- I would need you to walk toward me like this...

- I would need you to touch me like this...

Remember, they can show you what they mean with their body, they can adjust your body, and they can even give you micro-corrections like: slower, faster, softer, harder, yes, etc.

Spend no more than 3 minutes on Part I, and then move on to Part II.

Part II. Turn on your partner in 90 seconds

Now that you know what they want, you have 90 seconds to deliver the goods. It's very important when you are on Step II that your partner is no longer coaching you. If your partner tries coaching you during this time, it will more than likely ruin the practice. Instead of verbal coaching, what your partner can do is sound how you are making them feel in real time. By only using the "mmm" sound they can express either a "yes" ("mmm" like a purr) or a "no" ("mmm-mmm" like an eww) just by the way they sound it. Be sure that feedback is limited to "mmm" sounds only in Part II.

Remember, you and your partner are on the same team. You want them to succeed and they want you to succeed. So always think of your "mmm's" like a compass, pointing your partner toward your true north. Even when they get the slightest thing right, use a positive "mmm" of encouragement to let them know they're heading in the right direction. If you withhold all positive responses from each other, it's highly likely you or your partner will become frustrated quickly and may even give up. You want to keep each other in the game, and you both want each other to get it right.

Part II is also where you practice receiving. If you have a partner who is willing to get to this point with you, that's pretty amazing. Anyone who is willing to learn how to love you better is a pretty special person. They may or may not be doing it well. However they're making an attempt and it's your job to receive it. Let it in to your heart. Breathe it into your body. Soften into the moment and receive your partner's attempt fully.

After the 90 seconds is up, break all physical contact, return to a neutral position and move on to Part III.

Part III. Receive your partner's feedback
Once back in a neutral position, re-establish eye contact with your partner, gazing into their left eye, and before you say anything...

*** *Breathe* ***

Next they are going to give two very specific pieces of feedback:

What I loved most about that was...
Even if it didn't go so well, there needs to be something about what you did that they loved. They could love your effort. If it went really well, your partner should let you know everything they authentically loved about the experience.

What I would need more of is...
Even if it was perfect, there needs to be something that could be improved upon. This is required in order for your intimacy to deepen. Every practice can be improved upon. Maybe it's just one thing like needing you to keep more eye contact, breathe deeper, make sounds or move more. Or maybe it's many things, and if it is, it would be best to limit the amount of feedback to only three adjustments.

Once Part III is complete, if you still have time, go ahead and repeat Part II and Part III as many times as you can, until time runs out. This way, you are getting several attempts to keep improving. If you're both good at giving feedback, and not taking corrections personally, you'll both improve very quickly.

When the alarm sounds and the first 10 minutes are up, the first half of the practice is over, and it's time for you and your partner to switch roles and repeat Parts I, II and III.

After the final 10 minutes are up, and the practice is over, return to a neutral position with your partner with no physical contact. Re-establish eye contact with your partner, gazing into their left eye, and without saying another word...

*** *Breathe* ***

Take this moment for you and your partner to acknowledge that the practice has officially come to an end. You may bow to one another.

You may hug. You may smile at each other. Or you may burst into belly laughs. Whichever feels best to both of you is fine. What's important is that once the practice is done, there is no more feedback. Feedback is a powerful tool for development when used wisely. Used unwisely, like all things powerful, it has the potential to do more harm than good. Be mindful of the containers you create with your partner, and through them, you will most certainly deepen in love.

*To experience being guided in this practice, go to www.AwakenedWomansGuide.com/resources for an audio of Justin and Londin leading you and your partner in this exercise.

PILLAR III: DEVOTION

"Go to your fields and your gardens, and you shall learn
that it is the pleasure of the bee to gather honey of the flower,
But it is also the pleasure of the flower to yield its honey to the bee.
For to the bee a flower is a fountain of life,
And to the flower a bee is a messenger of love,
And to both, bee and flower,
the giving and the receiving of pleasure is a need and an ecstasy."

- Kahlil Gibran -

Introduction to the Pillar of Devotion

In Pillar I, we cultivate the ability to land in the right-now moment.
In Pillar II, we hone the ability to turn on passion at will.
In Pillar III, we awaken the ability to love without condition.

There are many kinds of devotion: you can be devoted to the divine; you can be devoted to a particular faith; you can be devoted to your family, a sports team, an art form like photography or dance, or a meaningful cause. All of these can be beautiful forms of devotion, but the devotion we speak of in this section is devotion to a sacred relationship.

- What if you became a living, breathing vessel for love-consciousness to serve another?
- What if you lived in mystical union and divine grace every day of your life?
- What if your love could open your partner to the divine?

This is what it means to live in devotion to sacred intimacy. Devotion allows you to deepen alongside another, no matter how much adversity life sends your way.

Devotion is important because it is the only way to feel truly fulfilled in love. All other paths will fall short. All self-centered practices will backfire. If we hold back our gifts, we lose. If we wait for the other person to measure up before we give our love, we wait forever. If we close our heart until circumstances improve, our heart will harden. If we hold back love in any way, we actively downgrade our relational dynamic.

The devotional way of life involves landing in something bigger than your own agenda. It is viewing your intimate relationship as a living prayer, knowing yourself as an agent of love, and opening each moment into greater awakened realization. It is the love you give without worrying about what you are getting back.

Devotion is a mindset. It is a decision you make. It is the hallmark of spiritual maturity.

In this section, we will explore the following aspects of devotion:

- Why the unbridled expression of your authentic heart is the greatest gift you could offer your partner.
- The important difference between devotion and manipulation, and why devotion has nothing to do with subjugating or suppressing yourself in any way.
- How living in devotion with an intimate partner will accelerate your growth more than any teacher, coach or guru ever could.
- The gifts Omega brings to Alpha and the gifts Alpha brings to Omega.
- How living as devotion while dating allows you to call in a sacred relationship.
- What to do when your partner feels unworthy of your devotion.
- How divine surrender can turn lonely isolation into beautiful lovemaking.

We'll finish by offering you an exercise to get you started on the path of living in devotion with your partner right now.

21

Relationship as a Living Prayer

Devotion allows us to approach relationship as a living prayer. In doing so, we experience our entire life blooming in a way that otherwise wouldn't be possible.

In sacred relationship, we embrace our power as lover to create the most delicious and profound life experience for another. Once we begin to see the positive impact we can have on our partner, we realize we are powerful agents of change in the world. We have the ability to improve life not only for our beloved, but for all of those people we hold dear. We have the ability to live life from our full radiant power, not just in intimacy, but in all we do.

In this way, we begin to honor our intimate partner as the greatest teacher we could ever find. Even though they can be challenging, they provide the most brilliant mirror for us to truly see ourselves.

Some people hire a personal coach to do this. However, the coach is limited to the appointment time and whatever content you bring to the session. With an intimate partner, all of you is on display at all times. They see the best and worst of you. It all gets revealed. Whatever has been hidden or held back has the opportunity to be seen, accepted and loved.

In the devotional path, two beings push the edges of love and consciousness together. They humbly realize neither of them could go as far on their own. Their partnership accelerates their growth dramatically, in all areas of their life.

A partner will teach you more about yourself than you could ever discover alone. In fact, they will reveal more than you even want to see about yourself. The road to self-discovery is a humbling one, and may force you to face parts of yourself that you would prefer to keep hidden under the rug for a few lifetimes.

However, each time your partner unearths a difficult piece, they help you break chains you didn't even realize were holding you back. When you stop playing the victim or blaming the other, and instead use what is happening in the relational field as your playground for growth, you begin to experience dramatic acceleration in your spiritual evolution.

You know you are on track with sacred relating if you feel like what is being asked of you is just out of reach, slightly out of your comfort zone. That's when you've hit the golden territory, the stretch that extends your reach and unfolds your fully embodied power. Just like a difficult yoga class will open your body, a sacred love relationship will open your soul.

This path is not for everyone. It's especially not for you if you are looking to learn techniques to manipulate a partner to get what you want, even if what you want seems noble, such as a house, marriage or baby.

On the other hand, if you are willing to un-guard your heart and love to the fullest, no matter how vulnerable it feels, this path promises to take you into unimaginable realms of magic. The reward is to know the living, breathing, felt experience of divine love, not only in your relationship but in life itself, through intimacy.

While giving love so vulnerably feels like an intense stretch, it brings profound gifts. Not only will it enable your intimacy to last for a lifetime, the devotional stance will improve the quality of your life more than you could imagine. By learning to show up to intimacy as your authentic self, you gain the capacity to show up to all of life with more potency. Your mission will clarify, your capacity to handle adversity with an open heart will expand, and your ability to manifest your dreams will strengthen.

Devotion is a beautiful way of living because we begin to see the positive impact we can have on another and our tribe.

From the Omega-playing role, we see we can awaken Alpha into deeper consciousness through the revelation of love-light displayed through our form, whether that is adorning the body, expressing the deepest heart's truth, or nurturing through pleasure, home and creative expression.

From the Alpha-playing role, we see that we can awaken our partner as Omega by providing vision, direction and clarity of purpose, being the protector, provider and ground upon which they stand.

When we offer these gifts to each other in a dance of energetic agility, we become better versions of ourselves and significantly more powerful forces in the world. Rather than our relationship detracting from our mission, it accelerates it.

- By learning to find our voice with an intimate partner, we learn to find our voice in the world, whether that is speaking our truth, setting boundaries, making more money or expressing creatively as an artist.

- By cultivating the ability to open when we would rather close, we develop the capacity to meet life's challenges head on.

• By seeing ourselves bloom in partnership, we gain the courage to let our radiance and power lead others.

Devotion Begins When We Embrace Living as Love

To live as a devotional being, we make a profound shift—we stop looking for someone to give us love and instead we embrace living as love.

When we get caught up in life's distortions and allow ourselves to lose touch with the divine, it will feel like love itself is abandoning us at every turn. A partner's withdrawal of love will make us feel like we cannot breathe. Their rejection will feel as though they are cutting us off from love's flow. In reality, this is never true. In the act of reclaiming connection to divine love, we realize we are love. We do not need to go looking for it, ever. No romance can give it to us. No comment or rejection can take it away. We already have the love we desire because we already are the love we desire.

This shift to living as love improves our relationship in profound ways. We stop waiting for the perfect man or perfect relationship to connect us to the flow of love. We live in devotion to love whether we are single or married, feeling good about our relationship or not.

We especially stop using love as a way to manipulate others. As we live in the unbridled expression of our heart's truth, we realize love has little to do with people-pleasing, being agreeable or subjugating our power. Instead we liberate our full expression. Love has many faces. In the act of living in devotion, we embody the full spectrum of love's flow, from angelic to fierce, light to dark.

Let's look closer at some of the orientations devotion invites.

Maintain a Beginner's Mind

The secret to longevity in relationship is to approach love with a beginner's mind. Forget everything you think you know about love. Never assume you know what love is or what it is supposed to look like. Imagine you have no idea how your partner needs to be loved, or how you yourself need to be loved. Because in truth, you don't. None of us does. The second we think we know what love is or what it's supposed to look like, we will find ourselves reducing love to only that which is familiar to us, whether it feels pleasant or not.

With the beginner's mind, we gain the ability to break out of repeating patterns which numb us to our lives. To break out of any unwanted habit requires you to step beyond the bounds of what is familiar to you. For example, to stop being a relationship cycler, you must learn to relate to relationship in a way that encourages longevity—something totally counter to the short-term approach you've been fixated on, which may feel comfortable and familiar to you but is likely based in a limitation you adopted in your childhood and have been operating from your entire life. This is why it requires the beginner's mind. Only in giving up everything you think you know about love can you enter into the territory of that which is new.

Love is infinite and it cannot be bound by definition. To attempt to do so is to literally limit the love that is possible in your life. It is only when you release the expectations reinforced by the familiar patterns of your childhood that you create the space required to experience something far more profound.

So if you accept that you don't know what love is supposed to look like, you'll never assume you know how the person standing before you needs to be loved. Instead, you can show up to every moment as if it is a new opportunity to experience love in a way you've never experienced it before. You can never know what love will have in store for you tomorrow or even 15 minutes from now. That's what makes it all the more magical.

The freedom lies in realizing we cannot escape love's embrace. Our longing is eternal and beautiful, not to be fixed or caged, but to be ridden like a wild horse. When the two of you share the same knowing, you are both liberated, free to face dark and light in full loving embrace, knowing there is neither something simpler nor more complex, neither more fulfilling nor more terrifying, than total surrender into love.

Walk this path with an open heart, so curious you can't help but be fully present. Feel everything, moment to moment, as if nothing were familiar and anything were possible. Embrace eternal yearning. Realize the ache is beautiful. It is the very gift we bring to our beloved—we channel it into devotion.

22

Living as Love,
Whether Single or in a Relationship

The idea of a relationship and "happily ever after" can be a subtle trap. It can become a fantasy we associate with our ability to live as love. And while a partner helps you deepen, a partner does not give you your connection to the flow of love—that is something you give yourself.

If you hang your ability to love on your partner, you will feel hopeless when they have a bad day and don't give you the love you want right then. Your connection to eternal love will be degraded to something transient, out of your control and subject to human flaws. You are way bigger than this: you are love. And the more you remember that you are love, the more you have to offer in a relationship. The more skillful you become at owning your connection to the divine, the greater your chance of calling a sacred relationship into your life—whether you're currently single or with a partner already.

It is the principle of polarity that in every moment you attract your reciprocal. If you are shrouded in fear, hiding your heart and shutting down your light, you will resonate men who wallow in powerlessness, dim their clarity and cannot keep their word.

To attract a man who is ready to live in sacred relationship, or inspire your current man into offering this depth of relating, you need to begin living the principles of sacred relationship—absolutely and unapologetically:

  • If you are single and wishing you were wrapped in a man's arms, could you meet your own heart so fully that your own longing for love blew you wide open?

  • If you are nursing a break-up, tempted to put up a wall of armor around your heart so no one ever tramples your tender garden again, could you soften your heart, allow your pain and find the part of you that is larger than any outside circumstance?

  • If you are in a less-than-satisfying long-term relationship, sitting on top of years of hurt and disappointment, could you open your heart again, no matter what?

You need to shine, radiate and emanate love-light. How you do this is to practice these principles first with yourself. Open your heart, embrace your yearning, feel your body, bring the sacred into your daily life. When you do, you attract a partner who matches what you are offering—real, raw, honest, unbridled loving.

It's easy to fantasize that it will be better when you have someone who is practicing with you, giving you all these qualities back as you bring them forward. But it is not true. Fantasy is a dead-end game, whether you are single or married.

You cannot control another person. If you have an agenda of any kind for what your partner is supposed to do, you are setting yourself up for serious frustration. This book is about letting go of an agenda, and learning to meet each moment for what it is, whether that moment is going the way you want it to go or not. It's about learning to give your love, no matter what. Sacred relating isn't about being in a fantasy. It's not about everything being amazing all the time. It's about making art out of every moment.

It is choosing to feel, embrace and fully live in the body through dark and light. This is how you shift into loving as the unguarded heart. This is how you learn to live embodied, through pain and pleasure. This is how you stay open to the flow of love that is available in every moment through your connection to the divine. This is how you show up to a man and teach him how to do the same. You are the leader of love. Begin leading yourself into love, right now, no matter what.

If you wait for things to get good before you connect deeply to the divine, your life will pass you by before you've ever had the chance to know the love you sense is possible. It is about connecting now. It is about giving the thing you wish you could get.

Offer Love, Not Manipulation

As we look at what devotion is, it's also important to distinguish what it most certainly is not. Devotion has historically been confused with some very dysfunctional qualities.

Devotion is not:

Codependency—The dictionary defines codependency as "a type of dysfunctional helping relationship where one person supports or enables another person's drug addiction, alcoholism, gambling addiction, poor mental health, immaturity, irresponsibility, or under-achievement." In intimacy, codependency shows up when people get confused about the teachings and start using the yoga to "open" (to say yes) to a man's behavior when what they really want to do is scream "Hell, no!" For example, an Omega-playing partner might put up with abusive behavior because she's eager to submit to being led. She settles for crap just because she's happy to have a strong man giving her guidance. This kind of behavior revolves around supporting a man's unconsciousness.

Devotion supports the awakening of his (and our own) greater consciousness. We are literally serving our partner by calling forth more integrity, not less.

Being a Martyr—Devotion is also not about giving from depletion. If you find yourself getting resentful or ending up drained, you know you are over-giving. When you do this, you encourage relational dynamics where the energetic exchange is a one-way street. Devotion is the act of filling up yourself first and then giving from overflow. In other words, your relationship to love is first with your higher self, by connecting to divine love in solo practice. Then, once you reclaim this perfect connection and nourish your spirit from love, you come back to relationship overflowing and eager to give.

People Pleasing—Devotion is definitely not doing whatever your man wants just because he wants it, subjugating your power to his, or in any way agreeing to things just to make your partner (or anyone else) happy. We are not suggesting you become one of those cartoon bobblehead figurines on a car dashboard whose head bobs up and down, constantly nodding yes to everything. Far from it. This is about being in your authentic "yes" and "no" without censorship. As a leader of love, it's about opening your heart so fully that you know the truth of the moment and express it without holding back.

Giving to Get—When acts of love or service are offered with an expectation of return, that is not devotion either. If a wife makes a fabulous dinner, puts on her finest lingerie and greets her husband at the door, that is a beautiful act of service—unless she is doing it for the sake of getting something in return. Let's say, for example, she wants to him to agree to take them to Italy. As they dine, she tells him about the trip she has in mind. He says they can't afford it and she goes into a rant, storming into the bedroom to put on sweatpants. Clearly the food and lingerie were designed to get him to agree to her dream trip. This isn't devotion. This is manipulation.

Offering love is never manipulative. But neither is it inauthentic or self-suppressing, even when it may feel less than pleasant to express or receive. It is common to associate love with sweetness, gentleness, and all things nice, but as we've started to see in our discussion of devotion, love doesn't always make everyone feel warm and fuzzy inside.

Embodying All the Faces of Love—from Angelic to Fierce

Sometimes the face of love is angelic, sometimes tender, sometimes sweet. Other times, it is fierce. It comes in as a rolling storm, which wipes out everything less than conscious in its path.

Love is not a weak or passive force. In the Hindu religion, the goddess Kali cut off the head of any man who was not fully conscious. Athena of the Greek pantheon is the goddess of war as well as wisdom. In the human world, think of a mother who lifts a car to save her child, or an activist who blows the whistle on political corruption. Think of women like Rosa Parks and Susan B. Anthony, whose love for racial and gender freedom changed the world.

In sacred relationship, love can look like presence and polarity, but it can also look like a wife calling her husband out when he is lying to himself, even if it feels uncomfortable or harsh, because she refuses to settle for less than his highest integrity.

This is the part of devotion that most people don't talk about. And it's probably the most important part. If you are worshipping the consciousness which comes through your man in his fullness, but he's not stepping up into that fullness of consciousness, it is your job as the leader of love to call him on it. It is not because you need to nag, shame or prod him. It is not because you are afraid, angry or frustrated. It is not because the relationship may be at risk, but because only you can demand his highest consciousness to meet your purest love-light. No one else can do this for him the way you can, not even himself. So if you don't call him on his BS from a place of devotion to his highest level of consciousness, no one else will…and that will lead to his never being able to meet you in your fullness.

Don't let that happen. Don't hide the fierce side of your devotion out of fear for what his reaction may be. If you are concerned you will be "too much" for him, remember responsiveness is what motivates a man. If you are squelching your fire, you are actually reducing his ability to meet you. The only legitimate reason why a man will tell you that you are too much is because you are either dragging him into past resentments, or dumping closure in his lap, throwing your emotions at him like a hot potato because you can't handle them yourself. Find the full expression of the right-now moment with an open heart and pulsating body, no matter how uncomfortable it may be, and you'll likely see him clean up his act and work like hell to be a better man for you.

It took me a while to understand this, even years into my relationship with Justin. As a child, my father left the room anytime I showed an unpleasant emotion. I loved my dad, so I learned to only show him the parts of me that kept him in the room—the pleasant, friendly parts. While this strategy worked well as a child, it backfired with Justin. Every time I felt anger and didn't show it, I went numb in my body. Every time I felt upset and didn't show it, I hardened up a bit. Every time I felt hurt by something he did and pretended to be cool, I gave him the mixed message that what he was doing was okay, when it absolutely wasn't.

Through my practice, I gained the capacity to show my anger and feel him receive it. In this awakening, I realized that feelings work like a pendulum. If I limit myself from swinging to the fiercer, darker sides, I limit my ability to swing into the experience of the lighter sides as well. In other words, the degree to which I suppress pain is the degree to which I suppress pleasure. The same is true for anger/joy and sadness/happiness. If I want to bask in all the "good" feelings, I need to allow the "bad" ones. Kill off the unwanted sensations, and the sensations I do want come in short supply. The body gets numb. The relationship stagnates. Life feels neutral.

In devotion to our love-flow, I began to tenderize my heart, show my emotions and, little by little, unleash the true me upon Justin. He learned, step by step, to breathe in my storm, not try to fix it, but to step into it and alchemize it into deeper loving. The result was my feeling an enormous amount of permission to express my fullness, which then led to the unveiling of incredible growth for both of us. The other benefit happened in the bedroom. By keeping my flow fully liberated, we were able to experience full-bodied passionate lovemaking at a new level.

Through His Eyes: Embracing Her Storm, by Justin

Sometimes the truth of my woman's heart can feel brutal. I usually get the truth when I'm least ready to hear it. Anytime I lose an ounce of trustability or waver along my path, she lets me know. Her response to my loss of consciousness cuts me like a knife…a really, really sharp knife—with a hint of poison on the tip of the blade.

It took me years to learn how to stay present with her in the midst of her emotional response to my moments of unconsciousness. I'm not just talking about basic anger or irritation here, but the full swell of her pure, raw, unfiltered emotional storms. It's in the moments when her emotions call me out, and grow to the size of a tsunami, earthquake and hurricane all balled up into one cataclysmic event, that I can feel my fight or flight response nervously scramble for the ripcord. Yester-years would've resulted in my anger, lashing back to keep her storm at bay long enough for me to make my escape.

That feeling of wanting to flee never goes away, even after years of practice. It's always uncomfortable. You can feel it coming like a cat sensing an earthquake moments before impact. And in those final moments, before the storm, my stomach twists, and suddenly, "boom!" She erupts like lava, spewing unbridled emotion from the core of her soul that stings, burns and blisters me from the inside out. What often hurts the most is the deepest part of me knows I've gone unconscious in some way. It is terrible to feel I have failed her heart.

In these moments, I witness that my first response is to treat this like an attack and to go on the defensive, but the yoga has given me the ability to pause, to respond instead of react.

I stop myself dead in my tracks, but I do not freeze. I realign my body in presence, softening with a full, strong, grounded breath which I extend beyond my body and into hers. My practice is fully engaged, but I dare not make it obvious, for that is the most fatal mistake of all. No movement can seem contrived—there must not be any attempt to fix the problem or quickly bring an end to the madness.

My gaze aligns with hers, my spine straightens, my breath becomes full - but all of this means nothing if I am not feeling into her. My inner voice screams, "Open your heart. Open your heart!" My nervous system resists, holding on tight for its own safety, certain that opening my heart in this environment is a bad idea. Standing with my inner voice, I do it anyway.

I see her. I feel her fully. Her chaos, her rage, her love, her hate, her fear, her sadness, her pain. I feel it all as my own. I breathe it in with her. We breathe it together. I stand in the eye of the storm, relaxing into the idea that it may never end—a vulnerable surrender intertwined with a persevering will, determined to stay in the moment as long as is required. It is here that equanimity is found. From here, I show up knowing there is nothing to be accomplished, fixed or changed, but to embrace this moment, fully present, committed and with a wide-open bleeding heart.

From here, I love her.

She feels seen. She feels me present. She feels there is ground beneath her feet, and that I am going nowhere. From here, her storm alchemizes into affectionate love as she feels I am with her in this moment.

It's never fun to be on the receiving end of your lover's feedback. But it is her heart's truth that sharpens me. It is her courageous reflection of my unconsciousness that awakens me. It is her full expression in the right-now moment that forges me into the man I am destined to become. But only if the two of us wield it well—with open hearts and fierce devotion to love.

Can you see how you do your man a disservice by holding back your truth and hiding your emotions? Your unleashing is your gift to him, but only when done with an open heart.

*** *Breathe* ***

23

Three Steps to Approaching Relationship from Devotion

Another distinction of devotion is that it is not something "to do." You just heard Justin say we are letting go of fixing anything or controlling outcomes. Rather, devotion is an orientation to life, a way of approaching intimate relationship on a day-to-day basis in full surrender. To live in devotion, the awakened woman adopts a devotional mindset and practice.

In our work with others, we have noticed that when a couple first arrives, they are generally holding a "What's in it for me?" attitude. This has a very detrimental effect on their relating. Once they achieve a level of maturity in sacred relating, they shift to a different mentality, one that sounds more like "How can I open both of us to the divine?" This is when the discord ends and the magic begins.

Here are the three distinctions required to shift into devotion as it relates to sacred intimacy:

1. Shift Your Mindset from Getting to Giving
2. Learn How to Open Your Partner
3. Cultivate Your Embodied Gifts

Step 1. Shift Your Mindset from Getting to Giving
On the devotional path, relationship takes on a new orientation: we go from looking for what we want to get out of relationship, to what we can give.

We stop loving our partner the way we prefer to love them and begin focusing on what they require to be loved, not in a codependent way where we tap-dance around their kinks, closures and insecurities. We do this in a way where we know them in their majesty and help them become the greatest version of themselves.

Devotion is the one pillar that can't be practiced selfishly. You can practice presence and polarity in self-service if you want. You can read the first pillar and say, "Great, I'm gonna bring presence and get the attention I want from my partner." You can read the second pillar and say, "Awesome, I'll practice polarity and finally get the amazing sex I've been missing." But if you approach this third pillar of devotion from a place of self-service, it will blow up in your face. And that's why it's so powerful. Devotion must be selfless. And in being selfless, it helps us learn to approach presence and polarity selflessly as well. This union of powerful practice with selfless service is what actually makes a sacred relationship work.

This gets intense when it confronts and stretches our comfort level. The thing I feel Justin needing from me to be his best self always seems to be the thing I'm having trouble with—not because I'm not capable, but because it's the exact thing I'm resisting due to my own closure or wound.

It makes sense, right? Where I'm already liberated, I am already bringing my full self to the relationship. Where I'm shut down is where I'm resonating him into a shutdown as well.

For example, after I had recovered from a string of difficult miscarriages, there was a lingering side of me that felt flawed and over the hill. I had lost that "maiden energy" I once brought into our dynamic, where I felt bouncy and sexy and full of potential. The miscarriages beat it out of me, making me feel old, deadened and used up. I could tell Justin really missed the flirtatious, light, sexy sides of me. He would say to me, "Where is my girl? I miss her." When I went to find these parts of myself which had gone missing, I had to face all the limiting beliefs that had come up from those tragedies, all the ways I had given up on myself, all the ways I felt old and ugly and unworthy—just to reclaim the bouncy, light-hearted part of me that lights Justin up and turns him on.

It was one of the toughest emotional journeys I've ever taken. But eventually I did find that authentic thread of bouncy light, and it was like a breath of fresh air for Justin—and for me. A part of me was back that might have forever died. On my own, I don't think I would have ever fully recovered, because without Justin's devotion I would never have noticed that part of me was gone in the first place.

It was so powerful to discover that the thing that Justin needed was actually the thing that I needed as well. This is the truth in sacred relating: it seems like it's about your partner, but it's almost always about yourself. Your partner simply shows you the places where you are playing small, disempowered or otherwise compromised. When you liberate those places, and see your partner light up, you realize your full potential as a lover is back and that is exhilarating for both of you.

Through His Eyes: Shards of Glass, by Justin

I've spent the majority of my life cultivating the ability to empty my mind and experience equanimity in practice. The peaceful emptiness nourishes the Alpha soul. However, the very nature of relationship is far from empty and peaceful. Choosing to be in relationship with a love-driven being means her fullness will invite a whole spectrum of feelings and drama into the picture that otherwise wouldn't be there. When Londin is happy, it's like adding color to an otherwise black and white world. When Londin is in pain, it's brutal, like shards of glass cutting into my heart. Never was that more true than when Londin and I faced her series of miscarriages…

For more days than I could count, I would lie with Londin, my belly pressed into the small of her back, one hand on her stomach, the other on her heart. Her tears would pour eternity as she bawled in my arms. Fear took intense hold of me as I seriously considered the fact that her sadness might never end. Another child lost, this time at 20 weeks, and with it had gone every ounce of Londin's joy.

Only years of practice allowed me to breathe with her through the pain. Every breath she took, I took it with her—mine synchronized with hers. I was breaking internally. It seemed nearly impossible to sit with so much emotion, with so many tears, so much pain, for so many months. I wanted desperately to escape, to find a way to crawl out just so I could go back to feeling nothing again, but I refused to leave her side. Every breath was more painful than the last, yet I continued to practice. It felt as if I was breathing in shards of glass as the trauma began to build spiritual scar tissue inside of my body. But I refused to let her feel all of this alone.

It's in moments like these, when I make a conscious decision to stay present and keep my heart open, no matter how difficult the moment may feel, that have fostered our love into something so deep where I feel her heart as my own.

Step 2. Learn How to Open Your Partner
Once we shift into an orientation of giving, the next step is to hone our ability to give.

Sometimes people give in ways that actually shut down their partner. Have you ever seen a man who is super excited to tell his woman all about his new business idea...and an hour into his non-stop babble, she is falling asleep at the table? This is what it looks like to give in a way which actually closes your partner. While he is giving his enthusiasm and trying to create connection, it's not landing; it's ruining the flow of intimacy rather than increasing it.

If what you're doing doesn't open your partner, no matter how lovingly you mean it, all you're doing is loving them the way you want to, not the way they need to be loved. This is not true devotion.

In this step, we learn how to give in a way which opens our partner, creating an intimate moment that is tantalizing for both.

Everyone is capable of being inspired or challenged in such a way it motivates them to make a shift. The trick is how skillfully that feedback is delivered.

- Did it produce the result both of you were seeking?
- Did your partner become more conscious or less conscious after your feedback?
- Did they embody more or less love?
- Did their body open or close in response?

You must know these answers to be effective. You must become aware of your lover's responses if you are ever to truly serve them into deeper states of intimacy. The best way to navigate opening our partner is to learn how to interpret their body language from moment to moment.

Body language is one of the primary ways you tell how you are affecting your partner. Often, body language can reveal more than the spoken word, as it can be difficult for most people to share what they are feeling, especially in sensitive moments. But if you know how to read a few simple cues, the body never lies.

Here are examples of what it looks like when your partner is opening:

- They might take in a deeper breath.
- They may give a subtle sigh or "mmm" of relief.
- Their eyes may open wider.
- The front surface of their body may turn toward you.
- They may cross their legs toward you.
- They might crack a smile (even slightly counts).
- They may uncross their arms or take their hands out of their pockets.
- Their shoulders may pull back.
- They might lean in closer.

In other words, you notice your partner brightening, looking happier to be alive, feeling more present with you.

Here are examples of what it looks like when your partner is closing:

- They might breathe very shallow or even hold their breath for a moment.
- They may give a subtle "ugh" or "eww" sound.
- Their eyes and face may squint.
- Their head may slightly turn away from you.
- They may break eye contact with you.
- They might turn their body away from you.
- They may cross their legs away from you.
- They may frown.
- They may cross their arms or put their hands in their pockets.

- Their shoulders may round forward.
- They might take a small step back from you.

In other words, you notice your partner withdrawing, turning their attention away from you, becoming less present or shrinking in size.

Whether in intimate sexual occasions or daily life, the inquiry remains: Is what I'm doing degrading the flow of love, or magnifying it?

Now let's try putting these ideas into practice. What is one thing you could do right now that you think would open your partner or a loved one?

Write down your answer.

_____

_____

_____

_____

_____

_____

_____

_____

_____

_____

_____

_____

_____

Now go do it and come back and write down the result—how did it go? What did you notice in their body language? Did they open or close? How could you tell?

Write down what you noticed.

If it worked, great. If it didn't work, do not be discouraged. This is often the case. Feel the part in you that might be frustrated or let down, and know that to continue giving through your failure is the practice. If you can show up to that, you are now understanding what true devotion is. The moment you stop giving your love is the moment sacred relating comes to an end.

Step 3: Cultivate Your Embodied Gifts

The third way to bring devotion into sacred intimacy is to use your solo practice to cultivate the gifts you bring to your relationship.

When Omega rests into her majesty, she becomes the full spectrum of life itself—she is creation, thus she represents all of creation. To liberate all aspects of one's love-light is a tremendous gift, not only for your own life, but to your Alpha-playing partner as well. Here are some places to start in terms of exploring the full range of Omega's embodiments:

> **Untame Yourself.** What if you gave yourself permission to stop being so damn polite, well behaved and agreeable, and let yourself reclaim the wildness that lives in your essence?
>
> While most women are afraid of being told they are "too much," the truth is most of them are actually making themselves too little, too small and too powerless, and that doesn't work for most men. The fullness that comes from the liberation of your wildness is ecstatic for an Alpha-playing partner. This is because, in the sexual occasion, Omega brings the energy while Alpha brings the structure. When you, in your Omega solo practice, re-awaken your uncensored truth, you release a flow of energy which is naturally polarizing and full of sexual charge. Bring this flow to the next intimate encounter and watch his eyes pop out of his head.
>
> Never settle for subduing yourself again. Let your full expression be a gift for both of you.

Juice Up Your Pleasure Bunny. What if you gave yourself permission to reclaim your sexual desire as well as your sassy, strut-around-the-house-in-a-sexy-outfit self?

You are never too old, too fat or too tired to bring sexy back. More importantly, you cannot expect your man to do this for you. While he can help you feel sexy and have an orgasm and all of that good stuff, you don't want to have to rely on him to take you from zero to 60. Who has time to make love for so many hours anymore, where he could take you from numb to full-body orgasm? You never want to get to the point of feeling like a stalled car he's got to push up a hill. It isn't likely to happen.

What I recommend to my clients is to do enough solo practice they know their yoni (vagina) inside and out. They know what they like, what gives them pleasure, and they know what doesn't work for them. Most importantly, they are never very far away from their partner's touch sending chills up their spine.

If you want to be a good lover, you must find a way to buck the trend of sitting at a computer all day, and find your pleasure bunny.

Take the Seat of the Oracle. If you're willing to show your partner the full display of your authentic heart, whether it's pain or pleasure, he gets to see the impact of his consciousness in the world. This is what it means to become his Oracle. And what's so beautiful about you becoming this level of Oracle for him is that he gets to know when he's off course long before the world shows him he's off course—long before he starts running into problems with his business or losing the trust of his children. Your body lets him know when he's meeting life fully as consciousness and when he's slipping.

Your heart and yoni are incredibly sensitive tissues. They feel when something is off long before your mind can possibly track what is happening. Connect to them and you tap into the intuition which lives within your body. Intuition is defined as "the ability to acquire knowledge without proof, evidence, or conscious reasoning, or without the understanding how the knowledge was acquired." This mystical wisdom is your gift to him if you use it wisely.

The only way to turn on to this level of intuition is to practice first with yourself in solo practice by melting your heart and connecting deeply to your yoni—from surface (clitoris) to deep (cervix). Use self-pleasuring as a way to awaken to the deepest parts of your body and become comfortable with fully expressing. Then bring this offering to your partner. You teach him how to love you better, and you do this not through lectures or nagging, but through allowing him to see how he is affecting you.

For many years, I ignored my intuition, waiting for outside validation or proof to confirm my "knowings." I bought into the fear that I was too sensitive and difficult for others. As a result, I went along with a whole bunch of crap that felt off to me. Inevitably, weeks later, I would see my intuition had been right on the mark. So today, I listen. I trust my intuition and let it guide me. Justin honors my intuition too, and helps makes sense of it all for me. I bring the truth of my heart and yoni. He brings the clarity of consciousness. Together we live in sacred relationship.

24

Another Brick in the Yoni Wall

As you may have gathered, Omega essentially faces two options in every moment: stuff her true feelings down inside of herself, or offer them as a gift to her partner.

Here's the challenge. Hurts happen all the time. When we sensitize at this level, life can begin to seem like an onslaught of subtle and not-so-subtle jabs. Most women don't want to "go off the rails" and seem bat-shit crazy, so they learn to harden up, toughen up and numb out. They work to shield themselves from others so they can exist in a social world, but feel unaffected by the hurts which come with regular human contact. In essence, these women lay bricks around their tender hearts and soft yonis.

The problem is, lay enough bricks and eventually you have a big, nasty wall—a wall that not only shuts out hurt, but also blocks the majority of love-flow between you and your partner. This is how you end up sitting across the table from your man a few years in, feeling your heart hardened and body numb, dead all around and disconnected from desire.

Granted, when you decrease sensitivity, it is much easier to move through life without getting upset, losing your composure, or facing the heartbreak of how often you are let down. While it's not advisable to share these intense emotions outside of your intimate relationship, it's so important you stay in the open flow of expression with your man.

Stuffing your emotions has terrible side effects. Block your ability to feel, and it's harder to land in the right-now moment. Thicken your skin and your body becomes as dense as Alpha, reducing polarity. Harbor resentment and it becomes difficult to find your place of devotion. All three pillars collapse under the weight of this brick wall. And behind this wall, you are left feeling unmet by love and life.

Can you see the conundrum? It hurts to feel. But it hurts even more to not feel.

To truly embrace sacred intimacy, you must fully embody your authentic responses and feelings, and let them be shown through your entire body. It might make you seem crazy, possibly unenlightened and maybe even terrifying. But the payoff is worth it. You get to walk around with a wet pussy, full heart and wildly passionate soul.

Our client Alina had a major breakthrough around a similar pattern…

Love Conflict #8: No Orgasms for Alina

Alina and her man Dillan used to have spectacular sex, but over time their sexual connection faded and they ended up face down in the gutter of neutrality. By the time she came to us, Alina was totally repelled by him. Sex was incredibly unpleasant. She often felt stinging, terrible pain when Dillan entered her, even though her OB/GYN told her there was nothing wrong. Alina craved connection with Dillan, but when he was inside of her, she found herself counting the minutes until he came. Alina wondered what the fuck happened to her once-thriving sex life. She came to us because she didn't want to slide into old age devoid of pleasure and unfulfilled romantically.

Love Solution #8: Tear Down the Brick Wall

Alina first needed to recognize that she had a massive brick wall in front of her heart and yoni and that wall was drying her up, making her numb, blocking her ability to enjoy sex, and even making it painful for her. To enjoy sex again, she needed to tear that wall down.

We helped her start this process by re-establishing her solo practice, re-sensitizing herself, brick by brick, to her tender feelings. Once she was flowing again, she was able to figure out why she had put the brick wall up in the first place. Dillan had betrayed her several years earlier by cheating. It was so traumatic to Alina that she swallowed all of her negative feelings before she even consciously registered them. By not expressing her true pain, Alina never got the chance to unleash the hurt she felt at the betrayal. Alina literally "ate" her anger and sadness. Her stuffed feelings became the mortar she used to make her very large brick wall. By doing this, she not only lost the ability to feel pleasure, she also failed to give Dillan the chance to make it right, using her brick wall as a way to cope with a relationship she no longer trusted.

We met with Alina and Dillan together and facilitated a series of sessions where Alina was given permission to unleash all of that stored gunk. Justin instructed Dillan on how to receive her storm and not collapse. Together, they unearthed a whole bunch of crap that was sitting on top of their once-juicy connection.

After all of that was cleared, Alina and Dillan were able to feel the passion they once held for each other again. They were able to step forward in their relationship fresh, free of the chains of the past, back into the right-now moment and able to reclaim the devotion they both carried for each other. And most importantly, they were able to rediscover their sexual connection without any physical pain.

You don't have to be the victim of cheating to feel like Alina. Even small hurts can add up to big walls, especially over time. The takeaway here is to never allow your heart and yoni to go hard. I invite you to dedicate yourself to loving so fully that you express your feelings to your partner, not because you unload your crap, but because you refuse to allow a single brick to form. In other words, you express for the sake of the full flow of love to exist for both of you.

The price of the brick wall is immense, not only on your relationship but in your life. Your sexual energy is your creative potential. You shut down to your man, and that shutdown will extend to more areas than the bedroom. Because you spend so much time with an intimate partner, shutting down to them will require you to shut down in a big way in your life. It will have the sad consequence of reducing your ability to make money, know your deepest truths and manifest the goodness you want across your entire life.

That said, free expression is not always an open-hearted sacred offering. Sometimes we are carrying our own toxic crap and we are better off working it out in solo practice. Let's look at another example.

Love Conflict #9: Sara's Mind Gets the Best of Her

One evening, Sara's husband Mike unexpectedly disappears for several hours. Sara tries calling several times, but Mike's phone goes straight to voicemail. Her heart sinks into her chest. At first, she feels fear and concern for him. Then her mind begins going to worst-case scenarios—spinning stories that Mike might be seeing someone else. Sara loses trust and the stories in her mind send her into a full panic.

When Mike finally returns home, Sara meets him at the door, fuming, heart closed and on the offensive. Before Mike has a chance to explain himself, Sara begins spitting venom at him, demanding to know where he's been and who he's been seeing. Mike, having just dealt with several hours on the side of the road, his car broken down and phone dead, just wants nothing more than to collapse into Sara's arms and forget the whole ordeal. However, being met at the front door with anger and suspicion is the last straw for him. Completely exasperated, he turns around and walks right back out the door without saying a word.

Sara breaks down sobbing. The abandonment she was so afraid to experience is now happening in real time.

Love Solution #9: Listen to the Heart, Not the Head

Sara's intention to awaken Mike to the pain he was causing her wasn't inherently wrong. But it failed miserably because she made two major mistakes in her approach.

First, she jumped to conclusions. She created stories in her mind, shut down her heart and then threw her reactive feelings at Mike like a hot potato. If Sara had taken a moment to check in with herself, she would have realized she was disconnected, stuck in her head, and laying bricks of suspicion instead of listening to the wisdom of her heart and yoni. Her panic came from the false conclusions she was spinning in her mind—that Mike was having an affair versus having car trouble.

Second, Sara went on the attack. She laid her accusations on him without landing in the right-now moment, without feeling the truth of his heart, and without checking in with the parts of her body which can feel beyond petty fears.

If Sara had paused for a moment and checked in with herself, she would have realized that she was closed and pushing Mike into a matching closure. If she had stayed open in that moment, and felt what was true in her heart, she would have realized it was fear, not anger, that made her want to lay bricks. Anger came from the stories. If she had showed Mike her raw panic without jumping to conclusions, her vulnerable opening would have invited him into an equally open space. He most likely would have wrapped his arms around her and told her everything was okay. This would have been the exact moment they both needed to return to love.

It took me a long time to learn this lesson. In the beginning of my relationship with Justin, because I loved him so deeply, I would let my mind spin endless stories of potential loss, then come at him hard with accusations. Once I learned to check in more with my body than my mind, I was able to soften and express my heart. This is when our love connection went through the roof. Moments which had previously created separation between us became some of the most profound opportunities to bond deeper.

When we talk about unleashing, it is important to remember that we are unleashing to awaken our partner, not to dump our bad mood in his lap or drag him through the mud with our misery. When we have emotions unrelated to our partner, that is what I call homework. It's our job to unravel those pieces on our own in solo practice—not let them turn into more bricks in the brick wall around heart and yoni.

This is how it works in open-hearted sacred relating. The truth of the moment doesn't get lost inside of reactive patterns. If you close and go on the attack, you will resonate your reciprocal, pushing your man into equal closure, and boom, a fight erupts and everything collapses.

Your impulse to share your heart is never wrong, but your skillfulness in going about it will determine the growth and connection that is able to come out of such moments…or not.

It is how you handle the tough times, the times where you feel as though you are dying, which make or break a relationship. They are a fork in the road:

• If you choose to close, love loses, game over.
• If you choose to open, love wins and sacred relating continues breath by breath, day by day.

Closure

Shutting your partner out, either subtly or overtly, is closure. It could be as subtle as stopping breathing, disassociating from feeling your emotions, hardening your heart or not talking. It could be as overt as picking a fight, throwing a tantrum, attacking his character or in any way creating distance through drama.

Opening

Feeling your heart's authentic truth in the moment, and allowing it to move through your body, uncensored, by staying full in your breath and unrestrained in your expression, is opening to your partner. In other words, showing him exactly how you feel in the most vulnerable way possible. Maybe it's sadness, maybe it's anger, and vulnerably displaying that as an invitation into deepening is opening for both of you.

It is the choice to open ourselves to love in each moment, no matter how difficult, that defines our spiritual maturity as a love-driven being. For us to stay open requires us to land in something much larger than our small self, childhood wounds or ego-centric fears. It requires us to land in devotion.

If you want your intimacy to look like passionate, unconditional, fearless lovemaking, then practice a lot of passionate, unconditional, fearless lovemaking.

25

Offering Devotion as Love's Light

The awakened woman devotes herself to solo practice. She stays committed to busting through the brick walls that form daily around her heart and yoni, and juices herself up with divine love. This is what allows her to be a powerful uplifting force for everyone with whom she interacts. It is also what allows her to enjoy a fully loaded, sensually fulfilling, sacred relationship.

Your sex drive is like an engine. If it idles for too long, it will turn off. Keep the engine revving by making time each day for something juicy and pleasurable. This could be a morning tea ritual, an evening bath ritual, or even a new twist to your shower time where you take a moment to feel the water sluicing deliciously over your skin.

Let all of this move you in the direction of making time for the one thing that makes life worth living—juicy love.

Take a moment to make a pledge to yourself. What are you willing to commit to doing for the next week to soften into the love that lives at your core?

Write down your pledge.

This is a question you could ask yourself every day for the rest of your life. If you want to be with a deep man, it is imperative you are living this way. You recognize he's deep because he's meeting life courageously and is committed to growth. He's going to require a woman who is the embodiment of radiant love to the equal and opposite extent he is the embodiment of consciousness (and vice versa). To reclaim these Omega qualities, which live inside of you, it starts with setting aside a little time each week to cultivate your gifts.

Needing Love vs. Worshiping Consciousness

If loving someone this much left you hurt in the past or you have a big fuck-you of harbored resentment for your man (or men in general) bubbling under the surface, devotion can get tricky. However, it is important to remember, devotion has nothing to do with earning love or adoration. If you try to do any of the things we will teach you in this book from a desire to be loved, you'll likely feel rebellious and resentful. Do them from true devotion and you have an entirely different story.

The things we are teaching you in this book will please your man. In fact, I've had many clients feel a sense of shame when they see his exuberant delight at receiving Omega. They wonder if they are selling out on the freedoms they fought so hard to gain as they use their "feminine wiles" to influence their man. They fear, in pleasing him, that they might be taking the women's liberation movement backwards. They are tempted to shut it all down and relate to him from Alpha-Alpha for the sake of being respected.

Don't fall for that. Remember, you can please a man from one of two places:

> 1. You can please him because you want to be adored and let all of your actions stem from the fear of losing him, or

2. You can please him because you worship the consciousness that comes through him and have all of your actions be in service to inspiring the greatness you know he is capable of bringing to all areas of his life. As one of my teachers would say: we are not worshiping the man, we are worshiping the consciousness that is coming through him.

In other words, your man has his good days and bad days. Just like you, he's not always worthy of worship. When you orient yourself toward worshiping the consciousness that has the potential to come through him, you rise above the, "now I'm in, now I'm out," mentality of love. You find permanence in your ability to stand by your man, no matter what.

Sacred intimacy in its best practice is love-light worshipping consciousness and vice versa. Omega is love-light and Alpha is consciousness. The most basic dance of energy—the one the entire universe is based upon—happens inside of you and your lovemaking.

The awakened woman shares power with men as an equal. However, there is a difference between you at work and you in your love relationship. When you are in your love relationship, you may want to be able to surrender to something about him. You will never be able to surrender to everything, nor should you want to. You have ways that are far more developed than his ways, physically, mentally and spiritually. This is okay. It doesn't mean he cannot trump your Alpha. The key is to find the thing he brings which you cannot, to find something about him that allows you to surrender, some dimension in which he is superior to you. Then use that aspect of him as a touchstone to rest upon and flow into Omega. Otherwise, like I did with my man-child, you will feel as if you are running the show all day at work and then running the show all night at home. Unless you like it that way, that just plain sucks. That is not energetic agility—that is an imbalance of power.

When you are the Omega-playing partner, you are breathing your energy through his structure. So ask yourself: do I trust his lead? When he is resting in his Alpha essence, do I feel inspired to worship? Can he trump my Alpha when it's time to switch the polarities? And on the Alpha side: does he worship your flow of love-light? When you are resting in your Omega essence, does he come to attention in presence?

If you are both cultivating something profound in each of your own practices, the answer to this can be a fully-loaded, juicy-hearted "yes" for both of you.

When Justin showed me who he really was, I felt that I definitely worshiped his essential nature. Even though he had very little money and was just out of college at the time we met, I felt the depth of his consciousness. I felt he had something to offer the world. Compared to the other men I was dating, he had less money, less accomplishments, and less clarity of path, but infinitely more depth. I could see this man was special and I felt like I wanted nothing more than to help him unfold into all he could be. His integrity was true at the beginning and has never once wavered in the many years we've been together.

To find the essence of a man, begin paying attention to how he holds himself in the world. Ask him deep questions which reveal his relationship to his purpose or his essential nature. These could be questions like "What do you feel you need accomplish before you die?" or "What would you lay down your life to protect?" Death is significant to men, so when you ask questions like this, you usually pull forth the deepest truth from his heart. Inquiries like these will reveal very important clues as to what drives him at his core. If he doesn't know the answers, that tells you he may lack direction or clarity. If he knows the answers, or can speak to work he's doing to find them, you just saw his direction and clarity.

How much I trust Justin changes moment to moment. How much polarity we feel with each other changes. How much willingness we both have to meet the moment changes. What never changes is how much respect I have for the man that Justin is at his core. The consciousness which moves through him when he is resting in his own fullness is a cock that I could suck until the day I die.

Justin isn't always "on." When he is playing video games, I do not feel in worship of that. In that moment, he is directing all of his awareness into a screen. What is there to worship in that? Not much. So I don't expect myself to worship it. But neither do I judge or shame him for it. If I was after my own agenda, I would nag him when he's in this place. I would insist that he come back to being a person who could lead me and fuck me open to the divine. Instead, because I stand in devotion to his fullness, I feel beyond my own preferences and into the moment. Maybe he needs a break and the video game gives him a way to empty his mind. If this is the case, I leave him be and let him regenerate.

Unleashing the Heart's Truth

Other times, though, it feels as though he is falling into laziness or avoiding something and thus behaving as less than who he truly is. I know this is true if it hurts me to be in the same house with him, if I feel like I don't trust him anymore, or if it feels as though I don't want to follow his lead anymore. In that case, I will unleash my heart's truth to wake him up.

He does the same to me. If I'm falling into closure with the way I'm showing up, he will let me know I'm suppressing my love-light.

It is not fun. If I'm avoiding something, the last thing I want to do is wake up. Truly, I hate him in that moment. I feel like a victim. I want to blame him for asking too much of me. But once I step into a higher place, I can feel he was right. Once I get right with myself, it all feels better and I thank him for showing me I was dimming my light.

Our mutual respect is complemented by our devotion, which demands the best of each other, not from complaint, but from true, unconditional love.

Can you see the perfection of this whole thing? Finding my flirtatious, happy side was difficult when I realized it was needed after my miscarriages. However, it immediately opened Justin when I found it. It awakened his consciousness, widened his chest and filled him with the force of Alpha. To give to Justin in that way forced me to rewrite a history which would have otherwise denied me the full bounds of my Omega radiance in this lifetime. It would have let the grief of the miscarriages win. Instead, by serving Justin, I served my higher self—I recovered my joy for life and got the true me back despite the tragedies.

Am I serving Justin or am I serving myself in this dynamic? In devotion, it blends together. We both grow from each and every moment, so sometimes it's hard to tell where serving another overlaps with serving ourselves.

When we reach that level of selfless devotion, we find it doesn't serve to overthink these things in the first place or to stress out over who is benefiting the most. In a relationship, we can spend all of our time thinking about what we want to get out of it and whether we are getting what we want. Or, we can recognize eternal yearning is endless and recall the more fulfilling questions: "How can I offer the thing I most want to receive?" and "What would open my partner right now?"

We take the focus off ourselves and our own neediness and recognize our power to give. When you have one person doing that, fulfillment is automatic because, in life, it's not about what you get, it's about what you give. When you have two people doing that for each other, you have the potential for magic.

*** *Breathe* ***

26

How to Stay in Devotion...
Even When Your Man's Behavior Sucks

In sacred relating, we are not talking about a fairy tale where everything always works out. We are talking about opening to love because we are love. There is a major distinction there, and it's this distinction that makes all the difference.

Your man won't always handle your emotional turbulence with grace. And he won't always behave like a hero either. If you rely on good times and good sex to be the thing that connects you to love, then you have a dilemma. Even in the best of relationships, sometimes trouble comes.

If you embrace your solo practice and maintain a strong relationship to divine love, you have the tools to deal with adversity. When he behaves poorly or becomes momentarily unavailable, it allows you to not go down the tubes with him. You are the leader of love.

Here are a few ways to keep love alive when it's not flowing with your man.

Take Space. During a time of discord, taking space is the last thing we want to do. Everything inside of us will want to fix things first, fearing that if we allow space, it will break us apart. I hear all sorts of fears from my clients when I suggest this: maybe he will meet another woman who gives him the energy he desires; maybe he will realize that he likes being alone better than being with me; maybe he will forget about me.

The fears throw up all sorts of reasons to not take space. Ignore all of them. Trust that space is excellent medicine for troubled times. In the space, you release neediness, reclaim your inherent radiant power, restore your connection to love's light and come back to well-being.

Allow Yearning. Once you have committed to taking space, the first thing you may feel is an increasingly desperate need for connection. Yearning will hit you hard. This is good. It is the pain you will use to make your way inside your body. If you have prioritized locating love flow outside of yourself, you may have a habit of squelching yearning rather than allowing yourself to feel it. You send a text, post on social media, start a conversation with him even if he's working—you do anything to create connection.

To find the liquid love that lives at your core, you need to stop pushing away the pain and start diving right into it. This step comes down to one thing: be willing to feel your ache for love's flow. Rather than reaching outside of yourself for a fix, let it pry your heart open, fuck you open to the divine and be the catalyst for the deeper, richer feeling of your own body and the connection to eternal love.

Surrender, Breathe, Move and Open. Yearning for love is what helps you find love. Feeling is the doorway. It takes you into your body, where you can tend to your needs and reconnect with your essence. When you allow your pain, you don't need to defend against it. All of that resistance creates what feels like a brick in your gut. Once you stop trying to hide from this gunk, you can take a breath with it, move with it and let it unwind. This will put you right into Omega's flow.

You cannot think your way out of these tensions, but you can move with them, breathe with them and integrate them. Once you have liberated that which holds you down, you will be able to reconnect to the reservoir of liquid love which is your essence. Pleasure will begin to bubble up and your entire body will fill with gooey love. Meet your man from that overflow and see what happens. As Carrie discovered, it is the key to reconnection with Alpha.

Love Conflict #10: Carrie Stuffs Feelings and Gains Weight

Carrie and her partner Tom had been together for seven years when Tom began taking a lot of space for himself. He stopped acting affectionate or interested toward her almost completely, which destroyed Carrie's world and made her fear for her marriage. She began to turn to food for love. Unable to face the weight of her situation, Carrie swept the anxiety under the rug by soothing herself with frothy lattes and crunchy snacks.

Nothing would fill the hole in her heart and Tom wasn't helping. When she would try to make plans with Tom, he told her he was busy. When she would ask to cuddle, he would pull away. When she asked him what was wrong, he told her he was fine. Nothing she did seemed to bring Tom closer, so Carrie kept stuffing.

After a few months of this behavior, Carrie had gained 20 pounds. She and Tom were barely speaking and her life felt like it was falling apart. She came to us terrified of losing everything.

Love Solution #10: Reconnect to Love

The first thing we told Carrie to do was stop paying attention to Tom's withdrawal and start focusing on her relationship with herself. There was no way she could inspire Tom to cherish her if she wasn't loving herself.

We helped her see how far out of alignment with her heart she had become through avoidant behaviors, such as eating to stuff feelings. For things to improve, Carrie needed to stop feeding the hungry ghosts that lurked inside of her, begging for scraps, and go for the real soul-satisfying nourishment that comes from rekindling her felt connection to love. She needed to stop numbing out, face her feelings, and let her pain be the doorway to opening her heart again, no matter how uncomfortable it became.

We helped Carrie start a strong solo practice to come back to self-love and reconnect with her body. Tears poured out of her as she melted the glacier which had formed around her heart. Each time a new layer came off her heart, a new layer came off her body. Each time she found the willingness to face her situation, she lost the desire to overeat. She started to feel more centered, grounded and capable of meeting life on life's terms.

Next, we identified how needy she had become for Tom's love. She was using Tom the same way she was using food—as a desperate attempt to fill the empty hole in her heart. This was unconsciously repelling him and pushing him farther away. From her desperation, every attempt she made to re-establish their connection was less about sharing love and more about wanting Tom to give her the love she couldn't give herself.

When she began reclaiming love as her own, independent of Tom, he suddenly started to take notice of Carrie again. When she began to reclaim connection to her body, Tom started to get flirty again. As Carrie stepped back into her power, her newfound radiance was mesmerizing and Tom was loving it.

Once she saw the dramatic effect it was having, Carrie became powerfully committed to her solo practice. Today Tom and Carrie are back in a good place. Carrie is back in balance, her marriage is back on track and her solo practice is stronger than ever. She knows it's the key to her happiness (and Tom's as well).

This is the process of coming to a relationship as an Omega goddess rather than a needy beggar. The takeaway here is to recognize that your neediness repels Alpha, while your connection to love-light and pleasure inspires Alpha. If you cannot handle the weight of your feelings and you go numb, you lose connection to the very thing that attracts Alpha in the first place.

Today, thanks to her consistent solo practice, Carrie has learned to be quite fluid with her feelings rather than stuff them down. When Carrie and Tom start to argue, instead of turning away to hide her pain, she turns toward Tom, softens her body and lets him see her vulnerable heart. Tom experiences this tenderness as an opportunity to step in and be her hero.

It is so important as Omega to do whatever it takes to stay in touch with your body and not turn to numbing out as a way to solve romantic problems. If you abandon your connection to your body, you literally lose the ability to meet another body in an inspired way.

It is the truth of your heart that's going to awaken your partner to what is truly going on for you. It is the truth of your heart that is going to have you stop settling for dynamics that destroy you. And it is the truth of your heart that's going to show you—and your partner—what is needed for difficult moments to resolve.

If you've ever felt your relationship hit a tragically rough spot and wondered whether it was doomed, take heart. In our experience, everything can change on a dime the minute both partners begin doing the yoga. We once had a couple come to a workshop who were on the verge of a divorce. They really didn't want their relationship to end, but they felt like they had no choice. As a last-ditch attempt, they thought, "Crap. We'll just go to a workshop and see what happens."

You could feel the seething resentment and hate between them. But when they stopped pretending and covering up the moment, when they started to show each other what was really going on, things shifted dramatically. She found the ability to emote, show anger and allow the full force of her flow to come back. He found the ability to meet her there.

The next morning, they came in to the workshop with these looks on their faces like they had done a really bad thing, and they were both delighted about it. When everyone asked them what happened, they revealed that the sex they'd had the night before was so intense, they had broken the bed at the hotel. It was like you were looking at best friends laughing at an inside joke together. All of the true love that brought them together in the first place was back, just 24 hours later.

What it took was for them to return to the freshness of their connection was the yoga. They stopped pretending and started being totally, utterly authentic. He stopped pulling away his consciousness. She stopped pulling away her heart. That is what allowed them to reunite in love.

I know when you're in this place, it can seem like there is no way out, but there is. The way out is to go extremely authentic. You have nothing to lose. Let the flow of energy come back between the two of you, and the flow of energy will do the magic on its own.

When you reclaim the divine aspects of yourself, you are able to once again lead as love. When you reclaim the Queen, you inspire him into being the King.

Through His Eyes: Excavating Her Heart, by Justin

One of the greatest gifts I've received in my relationship is having a woman who is emotionally current. What I mean by this is that Londin's emotions are not harbored over the course of years, months or even weeks. Together, we have created a relationship that permits the free flow of her heart's truth as it arises, and it allows me to know exactly where the two of us stand at every moment.

Once the feelings flow through her fully, I can feel her emotionally current with me, not harboring any resentments, anger or mistrust. To feel that in my woman is a gift I will always cherish.

Learning this skill can take time. No man will do it perfectly at first. There's an art to it. In the beginning, it may come off harsh, even overwhelming for your man to bear witness to your heart's raw, honest truth, but eventually, with practice, it will become a remarkable gift to the both of you.

It takes two to make this possible. It isn't just on Londin's shoulders. It requires me to be willing to show up to her truth, open my heart, stay present and let it in fully.

Another thing I have learned over the years is that occasionally, when something does get stuck in Londin, and she doesn't know exactly what it is, but I can feel it, I will invite the emotion out of her. I call this "excavating her heart." The minute I feel something stuck, I go in and extract it. This doesn't look like me putting a white-hot light over her head and demanding answers. It looks like stepping toward her, offering my presence and letting her know I feel something is there. I am patient with it. Sometimes it takes a little talking. Other times, I don't have to say anything for her tears to begin to flow. The emotion rises from within her, flows through her body, and once it is touched fully, the next moment is fresh and ready for something new.

I never imagined that this would be an activity I would enjoy, but it is. That doesn't mean it's easy, but the reward is well worth it. Once I felt what it was like to be on the other end of the clearing, it's hard to go back to that closed-hearted, secretive, harboring resentment experience ever again. Today, I do whatever it takes to have my woman fully congruent in her emotional flow. I know how good it is for both of us.

*** *Breathe* ***

27

Four Asanas to Practice Devotion Daily

We've talked a lot about how to show up in difficult moments, as a lot of devotion comes from how you respond to adversity—when your partner isn't stepping up, or when you want to close off to avoid feeling pain.

What we haven't talked about much yet is how to practice devotion in everyday life, when things aren't going badly but just going normally. Here are some tools which take regular relating into devotional relating:

1. Keep Humor In The Picture
In the commitment to continually deepen together, the practice can get very intense. Humor is the medicine that makes it all work.

Justin and I are constantly teasing each other, joking around and poking fun at our practice. At least once a day, one of us will crack the other up. It feels like water, washing the relationship clean and making everything shiny and new again.

Humor is a sacred gift that unsticks heavy moments, restores love and lightens the mood. Even tough times can be saved by humor. Many a dramatic discussion has collapsed into laughter when both partners are willing to laugh at the drama.

2. Give the Gift of Asking For What You Need

Sometimes the best gift you can give someone is to simply ask them to give you what you need. It is an act of devotion because you stop resenting your partner for not being a mind reader, and start being generous with helping them understand you better.

It is a beautiful freedom to be able to communicate what you need, particularly when it comes to things they could never guess, such as your darkest sexual fantasy. You can do this in fun ways, such as mailing him a sexy letter (even if you live together) or, in a moment of intimacy, seductively inviting him to touch you exactly how you need to be touched. To take something from emasculating to hot is simply a matter of how you approach it. Experiment with this and see if his body opens or closes.

3. Let Him Lead And Let Him Follow

For a man to lead, you must let him lead. The gift of having the restraint to stay in Omega and not jump over into Alpha the minute things feel uncomfortable is that you get a man who takes charge. I call this gap suffering his lead.

For example, let's say he says he'll pay the utility bill but he forgets. You can pay it for him or you can let the lights go out. Let the lights go out, and he'll probably never forget to pay the utility bill again. Most women do not realize this. They jump in and run the show the minute they don't like something. Their man feels emasculated, loses motivation and stops leading. The woman then wonders why she has such a useless man.

Conversely, it's important to take the lead when you notice your man needs a break. I see many women clinging to the Omega role out of fear they might get stuck in Alpha. I challenge you: don't let your fears run the show. Land in devotion and bring whichever embodiment best serves the moment—Alpha or Omega. If you do find yourself in Alpha, enjoy it, give it all you've got and trust that he's probably going to want to take the lead back before you know it.

4. Become an Artist of Love

Most importantly, never stop engaging with him, seducing him and inviting him to meet you in a fun, sexy place. No matter how long you've been together, treat each day like it was the first day of your relationship. If you are single, do this with yourself to stay buoyant and filled with love.

What is wonderful about sacred relating is it is all art. You are not treating your relationship or yourself as broken and needing to be fixed or perfected. Rather, you are loving yourself and each other breath by breath. You are using presence to land in the right-now moment. You are using energetic agility to bring polarity when you want heat, and resonance when you want partnership. And you are using devotion to serve each other's highest good and live in the flow of unconditional love.

This is what we mean when we speak of intimacy as an art. It is moments like these—dozens of them throughout every day of your lives together—that take you deeper into love. It is your willingness to show up as vulnerably, authentically, and unguarded as you can, even in regular, everyday moments, which allows for sacred relating to take place over the course of a lifetime.

Loving Beyond Intimacy

There is the kind of love we share with an intimate partner and there is the kind of love that transcends even intimacy. Each one of us uniquely longs to receive and give a kind of love that is not only exclusively bound to an intimate partner, but is rather an expression of the love we yearn for in every dimension of our lives. It is the love we ache for from our parents, the love we strive to share with our children, the love we experience when family and friends pass on and the love that fills us when new ones are born. It is our eternal yearning to be embraced by a love that transcends all time and space—a union with the divine.

For thousands of years, across countless cultures, the journey to know this kind of love has been written about, shared through stories and passed on through traditions. Whatever tradition we subscribe to, there is an inherent piece of wisdom that continues to reveal itself again and again as we contemplate what it means to live as one of the awakened.

Through our investigation, one thing becomes clear: there is inherent pain in the separateness we feel. No matter how much love, no matter how far we come, this intuition there is more to be had, more to be given, never goes away. The awakened one comes to the realization that this itch cannot be scratched, and that it is not supposed to be. Rather, it is this itch which uniquely defines who you are and your deepest gifts in love.

It is the singer who soothes the broken hearts of her fans with the songs she wrote when her heart was broken. It is the comedian who washes away the sadness of his audience with the jokes he wrote when he was overwhelmed by sadness. It is the scientist who heals the sick with a cure she discovered years after losing her mother to the same sickness.

When we are willing to see our wounds as a doorway into our greatest love offerings, and begin serving our relationship, our loved ones, and the world from this place, we get a taste of what it is to be awakened.

As awakened women, we live as love no matter what we are getting back. We stand by love and the truth of consciousness, reflecting courageously without concern of being rejected. Through this we awaken those around us.

The awakened woman loves not because she's rewarded for it or it goes well for her. She loves because she lives as love. She doesn't wait for someone else to give it to her. She offers it freely and thereby inspires those around her into the same place.

This is the essence of true love. It is the secret of the saints. It is the sorcery of the sages. This is the love that is written about in sacred texts and dreamt about in dreams. And if we look closely enough, it can be found all around us, permeating every moment, but only if we are willing to look.

You will never give your love perfectly. There will be times your greatest attempts will be misinterpreted, misunderstood or rejected completely. This happens to all of us awakened women. You cannot prevent it. But what you can do is you can choose to keep your heart open and continue to love fiercely, passionately and unconditionally, no matter what. No one can ever take that away from you. You can only take that away from yourself.

28

Feelings Rushing:
An Account of Divine Surrender

So what does it look like to bring devotion into the bedroom?

Let's look at a real-life example of a moment when devotion took me from collapse to ecstatic surrender, creating not only an incredible connection, but beautiful lovemaking.

With a pounding heart and a well of tears rising, I feel myself at a tender crossroads. I am not okay and once again, I want to give up on love. It all feels too intense, too overwhelming and too difficult.

I know in this moment, I'm facing a choice. I can stiffen up and pretend to be okay or I can show Justin what is going on. I hate showing him. It makes me feel so pathetic, so weak, so messy.

But, I'm devoted—to love, to Justin and to living the deepest experience I can in every moment. It's the thing that matters to me the most at this point in my life. And I know that if I were to listen to the voice in my head that tells me I'm in for a terrible let-down, I would dig my own grave. I would convince myself that the relationship is going to end the way all of my other relationships have—he cheats, he loses interest, he withdraws. I would be vigilant to avoid being blindsided. I would brace for impact and harden up so the blow wouldn't hurt as badly when it came. And that hardening would create the exact outcome I want to avoid.

It embarrasses me how much I love Justin. The vulnerability feels crushing. The intensity feels too much and I wish I had my shit together. I wish I were one of those girls who was cool, sassy and super confident. But I'm not. I'm just not. And to pretend to be so is a lie. It takes a complete lobotomy of my deep-feeling self to be so cool. That cutting off drains the juice out of my heart and yoni. If I do this, I dry up like a piece of hard fruit, baked in the sun. The withdrawal creates the discord I fear. It starts the minute I tense my body. Justin feels my hardening before I even intend to let on. And sadly, the cascade of negativity begins bubbling beneath the surface, Justin suffering as much as I am.

So yet again, I choose devotion, the same choice I've made daily for the past decade, the sole reason I believe we are still thriving together.

Out of devotion, I choose to show Justin how I'm feeling without holding anything back. I don't go hard. Instead, I go soft. I don't tighten, I relax. I get honest—brutally honest—first with myself and then with him.

I take time alone to get underneath my spinning mind and drop into a place that is deeper than my crazy thoughts. I feel beyond my tension and realize I'm dying inside. It becomes clear that my connection with Justin isn't as deep as usual and it's causing me to lose trust. I can feel my mind has been crafting stories to explain the distance. My mind has been wandering to old fears of whether I'm being betrayed, whether he's secretly fallen for another, or whether he's just simply losing interest in me. I realize in that moment that for the past few days, I've been in chaos, disconnected from the moment, from what I'm feeling, and up in my head. I've been alternating between telling myself I'm crazy, telling myself I'm right on, and telling myself I need to run before I get hurt. I've been listening to the voice inside that convinces me true love doesn't exist and I'm an idiot for believing in love.

As I continue to drop into my body, I feel the next layer. I feel the impact these fears are having on my body, tensing me up and shutting me down. The chaos of my mind is like a brutal taskmaster, causing me to lose touch with love and the light that normally fills my heart. As I look this fear straight in the face, it begins to lose its power over me. Tears of relief begin flowing. They wash away the tiring vigilance of my defenses. The walls around my heart melt and I can feel and touch what is under my chaos, which is my intense love for Justin and the crushing fear of losing him.

I don't judge this as unenlightened. I worked hard to love this much. I worked hard to be willing to be this vulnerable. I spent years reclaiming the willingness to care this much. So I continue to unwind until I am soft, flowing and wide open.

From here, I move to reconnect with Justin. I walk to him and show him the pain in my heart and body from our recent distance. I let myself dissolve the defenses I had propped up against him when I was listening to fear. I stand before him unguarded, undefended and unprocessed. The moment he sees this, he relaxes. I can feel the relief in his body. He has been feeling the distance as well as me. As soon as he sees the melting around my heart, the stand-off we have both been suffering is broken.

I can see him take a breath. I can see he can feel me like he hasn't been able to feel me in a while. His heart opens to me, his face softens and suddenly the current of energy between us is moving again. The glacier has melted.

He moves toward me, and stands a few feet away, like a mountain looking into me. I look back at him, letting him see into my breaking heart. The urge to apologize for my intensity is overwhelming. But I don't. Instead, I sink into his strength and feel even deeper, my heart unhinging. Even though we haven't even touched, we are already making love. He's sending his breath deep into my body and I'm sucking it in, letting it pry me open even further.

My mind wants to jump in at every turn, to talk things through and come to an understanding of why the distance occurred. I know this is a veiled attempt to cling to the safety of words, to reduce the intensity of how much I'm feeling in this moment, so I refuse. I release the need to speak, surrender my mind and let his deep breath penetrate my yoni and heart. I let myself be seen. I've never felt more loved in my life than right now, with him looking straight into my heart, meeting me in pulsating silence.

I love that he hasn't moved to touch me yet. It allows us to bond even deeper in the subtle realms, our bodies and hearts intertwining from afar. I live for these moments. They make the vulnerability worth it, and the surrender that was so hard to find at the beginning once again becoming something I would dedicate my life to offering.

He senses I'm to the point of yearning for him. My eyes are saying "take me, now," so he moves toward me slowly and deliberately. It's as if he's tracking my every breath to see if he's moving at the right speed to keep me dripping with anticipation.

When he finally reaches me, in what feels like an eternity of delicious waiting, he lifts my body up and carries me to our bed. I can feel his grounded strength holding me like a sentinel. I melt into him, my whole body softening. He pulls off my pants to find my pussy wet with the flow of divine surrender. My lips swell with anticipation for his entry.

He pulls his pants down to reveal a firm, erect cock. In this moment, I laugh at my adolescent beliefs that being "cool and unaffected" is what turns men on. With my messy heart unveiled, here I am staring at the truth of his arousal.

I feel my yearning all through my hips and thighs. My lower back arches, drawing toward him, silently screaming "Enter me, enter me, please!" He moves slowly, both deliberate and confident. I could explode with need. His maddening restraint sends my yearning into spasms of intensity. The same bloody yearning for love that was closing my heart in the last few days is now opening me to the divine, taking me into ecstatic explosions of full-bodied pleasure.

He places his member on top of my pussy. It rests like a heavy weight and I cringe inside of my demand. My lips begin to suck and squeeze for his cock. My fingers reach around his back to pull him into me, my face wet with tears gone by. I have never felt more alive and more loved in my life as he meets my mess with presence, and takes his sweet time.

Finally he slides inside. I gasp.

I am brought into the sheer pleasure of sensation. I want nothing more than to come immediately, but I remember my practice. I remember the yoga. I relax into the moment. I surrender ever deeper. I let the feeling of our union spread across my whole body. I feel into the place in me that is love. If I didn't know this place outside of him, I don't think I would ever be able to find it with him. I love him too much. I want to connect so badly, I would gladly leave myself behind. But I refuse this time. I want to know more. So I keep relaxing and letting the sensation travel across my whole body.

He whispers darkly in my ear and tells me to go deeper, open more...to surrender so much, open so wide, I have no bounds.

This is my favorite command. I live for this command out of his gravelly voice.

I do it and he moans. That single direction pulls me out of managing anything and the wave takes me.

My heart sucks his force deep inside of me. The rest gets foggy. It is waves and ripples and bubbles that spread and grow and dissolve and begin again. I'm lost.

He calls it done at one point. It's not done and I hate him for that, his fucking restraint. But it's delicious and keeps me at my edge in a way a completion never would.

I lie there splayed open mindless, floating in pleasure.

And then a few moments pass and the eternal yearning creeps back again as I begin to wonder, "Am I still loved?"

I have to laugh at my insanity, my never-ending demand. Fully embracing my insatiability, I let the incessant yearning for more pry me open even further, this time offering it to God.

When my call is heard, I am met deeper. My heart merges with the eternal, my body is taken into uncontrollable waves of rapture. I touch the place that sustains me deeper than anything else. I merge with the divine. The union melts all of my suffering. It fills me and everything makes sense again. In this moment, I know, this is the home of my eternal devotion.

Summary of Pillar III: Devotion

Devotion is the magic elixir which restores our ability to love without condition. Devotion will challenge you in powerful ways. However, devotion is what allows two beings to live as one no matter how much crap gets in the way. It unlocks our greatest potential, not only as lovers, but across our whole lives. The reward of the devotional path is knowing love beyond self. The devotional stance is the hallmark of spiritual maturity because it represents the ultimate liberation. It allows a person to get over themselves and their own petty agendas and begin living for the sake of the whole, to begin living as love. This is the yoga. It is the path of awakening.

As we showed you, you can live devotionally, whether you are single or in a relationship. All it takes is for you to begin looking at each moment of relating as an opportunity to create art, to offer the deepest expression of truth and beauty that is possible, for the sake of the person standing before you. In this way, we see beyond the illusion of separateness and we experience the embodied realization of two becoming one. This is the unicorn we are all seeking. This is what brings deeper meaning to life.

On this path, you realize that you can be the living expression of love at all times, in all places, no matter what. No one and nothing can take that away from you. You put an end to the "hungry ghosts" that roam around inside of your psyche making you feel like no amount of food, love or money is enough. You orient to giving and you feel fully met by both life and relationship. In long-term intimacy, you are also able to feel that there is a glue to the relationship, which makes the bond stronger than any challenge or adversity could introduce.

Devotion is the place Justin and I have been living in for nearly a decade, and I can tell you, it will challenge you in the grandest ways. Justin once said on the last day of one of our workshops, "If you think ayahuasca is crazy, try love." The entire room broke into laughter be-cause he was right. You may wonder why anyone would do it. But once you experience what it is to love devotionally, it's hard to imag-ine a life without it.

Pillar III Practice: How Do You Need to Give Your Love Before You Die?

For your final practice, we are taking you on a solo journey to discover how you need to give your love before you die. We asked you this question at the very beginning of the book. Now it's time to see how your answer has matured as you've deepened your understanding of sacred relationship.

This is a guided journaling exercise, so find a quiet place where you won't be disturbed and have a pen nearby. If you would like the audio version so you don't have to read as you go, visit the link below to be guided in this practice.*

Sit in a relaxed, upright position so you can go into a meditative state without falling asleep. Have these pages and a pen next to you.

Take a few slow, deep breaths, and let your awareness drop you out of your thoughts and into your body. Ease your mind, soften your heart and relax into your seat. Set aside all distractions. Drop into the right-now moment so fully, it is as if there was never another moment to be had. Use your Alpha skill of discipline to focus your mind on the visualizations we will guide you through. Then call upon the Omega skill of sensitivity to tune into your body and feel your responses to the questions we ask.

Let's begin. First, imagine yourself when you were a young child. A great way to do this is to remember a scene from your childhood home, school or playground. Whatever comes into focus for you is perfect.

How did you give your love? How did you meet each person in the exuberant expression of your authentic nature? Was it playful, adventurous, generously giving or unafraid to express? Was it overjoyed to dream about true love?

Take a moment to write down what you remember.

Each one of us knows this place. It's the place of innocent, uncensored expression. It's the place before our defense mechanisms came online. This light, exuberant, loving aspect of ourselves is our true essence. The more we can find it, the more we can remember who we are at our core and how we give love independent of the wounds of our childhood and the scars we carry from our lives.

Now consider what happened? Why did you stop giving your love in this way? What decisions did you make to hold yourself back? Were you shamed? Were you rejected? Did you get disappointed or feel unmet? Did someone violate your innocence? What happened that had you pull back this light in some way?

Write down your response.

Now look into your current life. Ask yourself what expressions of love have you held back from your current or past intimate partners? Is it generosity, trust, vulnerability, willingness to express authentically or permission to show how deeply you care?

Write down what you see.

This part of the journey shows you where you lost trust in giving your love fully. As we are learning, the problem with holding back our love is that we inspire others to do the same in turn. We attract partners who deny us love as much as we deny them love.

For example, he may be telling you white lies, but you are pretending to be happy when you are sad. You are both lying in your own unique ways. If you are guarding your heart, what is he guarding? If you are suppressing your sexuality, what is he suppressing? If you are hiding your authentic feelings, what is he hiding?

Now visualize your current or former partners. How did they hold back their love from you? What did you always want to receive that you never got?

Write down what you see.

Now look at your list from above. Do these withholdings you noticed match what you are withholding in some way, maybe not directly but similarly or reciprocally?

Write down what you notice.

What would it look like if you claimed your role as the leader of love and began to offer the love you wish you could receive? How would you love if you offered the love you spent your whole life waiting to experience? If you always wanted to be seen, how you could devotionally see your current or future partner? If you always wanted to be heard, how could you devotionally listen to your current or future partner? If you always wanted to feel unconditionally loved, how could you devotionally love your current or future partner without conditions?

Write down your answers.

Living from the devotional mindset, we stop waiting around for our partner to give these things to us and we begin giving them.

Now take it a step farther. What if you only had 30 days left to live? What if you had nothing to lose and no excuses for holding your love back? What would you need to give so that you could feel complete that you gave your love fully in this lifetime? How would you need to give your love before you die?

Write down your response.

As a commitment for the next 30 days, your practice is to give this love to your partner or loved ones daily. It could look like a certain touch, a certain thing you say, offering presence, offering your truth, etc. It could last 30 seconds or several hours. The most important aspect is, each day, to give others the love you wish you could get. Give it fully and without expectation.

The child loves from innocence. It doesn't have any idea that it could be hurt. The awakened woman loves from devotion. She has been hurt. She opens anyway. She lets no one and nothing stamp out the fire that burns at the center of her heart. She doesn't do this from going on the offense or in childish demand. She simmers in the maturity of leading others as love. She recognizes this part of herself is the most precious gift she can give. As she lives by this light in herself, she recognizes that light in others. With each person she meets, she sees the place inside of them that loved before they knew hurt and she calls this forth by modeling it herself.

The awakened woman is a powerful force for change. She is a lighthouse who turns on other lighthouses everywhere she goes.

As the last part of this practice, make an agreement, a promise to yourself as the leader of love.

- What are you committed to bringing the people around you?
- Who are you committed to being for the sake of love?
- What can no longer be broken in you? What transcends any circumstance, outcome or frustration?
- What part are you going to play on this planet as a leader of love?

Create a contract with yourself now. By signing on these line below, you're not only making a commitment to yourself, you are making a pledge to become part of a movement of awakened women fiercely committed to love.

Today, I, _____
(fill in your name) choose to live as love and offer my unconditional love and presence in these ways…

_____

_____

_____

_____

_____

_____

_____

_____

_____

Signature: _____

Dated: _____

This practice invites you into the true end of conditional loving, tit for tat bargaining and holding back for fear of getting hurt. I invite you to do this exercise seasonally, four times per year. Never stop revealing more of yourself, deepening inside of your commitment, or continual-ly unearthing new willingness to love at the level you did before you ever knew hurt.

*To experience being guided in this practice,
go to www.AwakenedWomansGuide.com/resources
for an audio of Londin leading you in this exploration.

CONCLUSION

Through His Eyes: Love Is Always Present, by Justin

Love is always there for us, pervading every moment of our lives. This realization is the holy grail of spiritual understanding. To find oneself capable of feeling love's presence in every moment is to achieve what some might call enlightenment.

Love isn't something we get from an external source, but rather something that lives through and in us. It is fundamental to our very essence as a living being. It doesn't need to be earned. It only needs to be realized. The same is true for consciousness, that part of ourselves which is always present. Whether we are sleeping or awake, sick or healthy, young or old, there is that part of us that remains eternally unchanged.

Love and consciousness are fundamental to life, and when we find ourselves resting in the awareness that we are both, life becomes a little brighter. It is the nature of waking up.

Ultimately, your journey is to awaken to this simple, universal truth: you are the Alpha and the Omega. You are both consciousness and love's light. You are the river banks and you are the river.

For whatever mystical reason, whenever we find ourselves feeling the depth of this truth coursing through our veins, we become alive. We sink into the moment, become present with our lover and our purpose, feel free and feel loved. It doesn't matter what is going on around us. We can find this place while we are painfully ill, suffering loss or struggling financially. No matter the emotion, no matter the situation, this realization is always available to us, our skill level as a spiritual practitioner is our capacity to know and live this truth...no matter what.

That's a tall order to ask of anyone. I get that. It's a tall order to ask of myself. But that hasn't stopped me from pursuing it ravenously, or walking that path alongside my lover. Once you taste it, once you get a glimpse that it is real, there's really no turning back. The greatest gifts we can give are to remain present with ourselves and one another, and embrace living as love without restraint.

When we witness this in another, something within us cracks open—tears fall, pins and needles shiver, and we feel like we are reminded of why we are here on this planet. If you provided this level of inspiration for your intimate partner, imagine how you would bring them to tears by the full force of your love.

How might your life be different if you decided to live this way? Would it be closer to living the life you desire most or farther from it?

In training myself and others over the years, this inquiry has guided me more precisely than any other I could ever ask. It has the power to help me see clearly by providing only two options: am I getting closer to the life and love I want or farther away?

The profound simplicity of this inquiry keeps me out of my head and in my body, heart and spirit. If I allow my heart to close after I've been hurt, is this closer to the love I want to have in my life or farther from it? If I storm out of the house and slam the door behind me, am I remembering the gift that is this life or am I wasting time wallowing in petty closures?

At every single moment, we have a choice to make. We can take one step closer toward love or one step farther from it. We can choose to become open and present with our partners or we can choose to close and shut them out.

Love is not one single emotion. It's all of them. Love makes us cry just as often as it makes us laugh. Love makes us hurt just as often as it fills us with ecstasy. It is dark and it is light. It is loss and it is gain. Love has no preference to any single emotion—only we do. And if we are stuck believing love can only be known in a single emotion, then we are missing out on the true depth of love.

Love moves. It is alive. It is present in every moment—no matter how dark or heinous a moment may seem. It is our capacity to recognize that love is present in all moments which demonstrates our aptitude as evolved, spiritual beings. And it is our duty in a sacred relationship to remind our lovers of this truth, again and again, so they may embody their fullness as love consciousness, and thus awaken to their greatest gifts in this lifetime.

This is the pledge we stand for. This is how intimacy and spirituality become one. They are one. They've always been one. And it is not our destiny to earn it, demand it or force it so. It is our pleasure to unwind the misguided thoughts, kinks, and closures, for the sake of knowing love's full force as it lives and breathes within and around us every moment of every day. It is our destiny.

Awakened Women, This Is Your Time

Now you have the tools for everlasting love. Putting them into practice is a lifetime process. Each and every moment is an opportunity to refine them. I have been at this for a decade and I'm still witnessing new childhood wounds, kinks and closures showing themselves. When they pop up, I open, breathe, soften, and love, no matter what. I do not let them convince me to close, cause a fight or shut down.

Each time I unwind an old karmic knot, a different one reveals itself. It is the nature of evolution. I don't try to get to a finish line. I have patience with myself and I know I'm untangling the karmic ball of knots of my entire lineage, and the collective as well.

Remember your job is to gently and consistently let love come through these knots. Breath by breath, moment by moment, it's about letting love meet each and every part of your body as new closures reveal themselves and you go deeper and deeper into the process of unwinding conditioning.

Justin is doing the same for himself. Together we are supporting each other unconditionally in this eternal process. We are each other's champion, looking only to see how we can love each other back into the moment. There are intense victories where our merger is magic, two bodies coming together as one in an explosion of orgasmic bliss. Other times, we endure the dismal sting of failed practice, where we suffer division, distance and hurt. We make room for all of it, not having to be perfect. Our only focus is to come back into the now, back into love, back into radiance and consciousness, all the while with devotion, two bodies merging as one in sacred union. Walking hand in hand, laughing at the mistakes, celebrating the victories and relishing our union, it becomes hard to tell the difference between the bad times and the good times.

As a woman stepping into my power, I treasure Justin's support. He is my rock. He shows me when I'm off. He shows me when I'm on. Sometimes I think I'm on and in reality, I'm horribly off. On my own, it would take much longer for me to see my folly. I believe this is how the patriarchy was able to sustain itself for so long—nobody on either side was calling bullshit on one another. In the new age, with a powerful partnership, you will have love and consciousness living in the truth of the other's reflection. The relentless mirror that is sacred relationship will keep you honest, open-hearted and well-nourished in the love of the divine. From here, you can create anything…and you will.

I wrote this book because I wanted it to be possible for every woman to awaken and thrive inside of everlasting love. Mind-blowing sex is a luxury I could not imagine living without. Feeling wild, unleashed and embraced in my emotional chaos is a heavenly home I could never forfeit. Being able to both kick ass in my mission and feel adored and beautiful in the eyes of my man is a gift I waited my whole life to receive.

Presence helps us let go of the reins and land in the body in the right-now moment. Polarity shows us how to keep things juicy, exciting and thrilling, even if we've been together our entire lives. Devotion helps us take on a selfless orientation from which all of this works. Without devotion, it's easy to turn against each other. Without polarity, you might have a deep connection, but no deep sexing, and without presence, you're still stuck in the mind and none of it is possible. The pillars work in tandem. They work on their own and they work together like a beautiful dance. We invite you to embrace the three pillars and consider, each day, how you could bring them into your life to become an artist of love.

Awakened women, this is your time. It's difficult to do this path by yourself. It's difficult to do this path with the counsel of friends in the old paradigm, cautioning you to love a little less, protect a little more and be enslaved by the limitations of your childhood wounds. I encourage you, create a community of sisters around you who are dedicated to living as unbridled love. Create a community that understands what it means to love like you've never been hurt, that supports your solo practice and rejoices in your depth. And as you do, call your man forward into greater consciousness, so he may meet you in the vibrational up-leveling of your life.

Justin and I are here to support you the whole way.

With Love,
Londin

Resources

All resources are available for free at
www.AwakenedWomansGuide.com/resources

Guided Audio Practices
The "Yes" Practice *by Londin*
Pillar II Practice: Turn On Your Partner in 90 Seconds
by Londin & Justin
Pillar III Practice: How Do You Need to Give Your Love
Before You Die? *by Londin*

Online Quiz
Polarity Profile Test: a free online quiz to help you find out
where you land on the polarity spectrum

For more about talks, workshops
and private coaching with Londin & Justin visit
www.LondinAngelWinters.com
www.JustinPatrickPierce.com

Contact us at **info@awakenedwomansguide.com**

26923029R00173

Made in the USA
San Bernardino, CA
23 February 2019